Series 3

Exam

Practice Questions

DEAR FUTURE EXAM SUCCESS STORY

First of all, **THANK YOU** for purchasing Mometrix study materials!

Second, congratulations! You are one of the few determined test-takers who are committed to doing whatever it takes to excel on your exam. **You have come to the right place.** We developed these practice tests with one goal in mind: to deliver you the best possible approximation of the questions you will see on test day.

Standardized testing is one of the biggest obstacles on your road to success, which only increases the importance of doing well in the high-pressure, high-stakes environment of test day. Your results on this test could have a significant impact on your future, and these practice tests will give you the repetitions you need to build your familiarity and confidence with the test content and format to help you achieve your full potential on test day.

Your success is our success

We would love to hear from you! If you would like to share the story of your exam success or if you have any questions or comments in regard to our products, please contact us at **800-673-8175** or **support@mometrix.com**.

Thanks again for your business and we wish you continued success!

Sincerely,
The Mometrix Test Preparation Team

Written and edited by the Mometrix Exam Secrets Test Prep Team
Printed in the United States of America

TABLE OF CONTENTS

Practice Test #1

1. Which of the following is defined as an organization that solicits orders for customers in the futures market?

a. Commodity pool operator
b. Introducing broker
c. Futures commission merchant
d. None of the above

2. Which of the following is TRUE regarding National Futures Association (NFA) registration?

a. Individuals working within the futures industry in supervisory roles must seek NFA registration as an associated person.
b. Individuals seeking registration must file an application directly with the NFA through the online registration system (ORS).
c. Firms doing business within the futures industry are not required to register with the NFA.
d. An individual's assigned NFA ID number will change throughout his or her career in the futures industry as registration is periodically updated.

3. The Commodity Futures Trading Commission (CFTC), in having authoritative jurisdiction over all commodity exchanges and their participating floor brokers, may do all of the following EXCEPT

a. monitor exchange activity for signs of price manipulation,
b. approve the terms of all futures and options contracts.
c. seek a restraining order against someone found in violation of their rules.
d. trade futures contracts.

4. Which of the following are always TRUE of a Futures Commission Merchant (FCM)?

I. They are members of the clearing corp.
II. They execute orders for customer accounts.
III. They must maintain minimum net capital of at least $1.5 million.
IV. They are required to file monthly statements of financial condition.

a. II and IV
b. II only
c. I, III, and IV
d. I and III

5. Which of the following is FALSE of National Futures Association (NFA) members?

a. Member transactions are limited to only those involving other NFA members.
b. To transact in futures with the general public, membership is required.
c. Members may not share commissions.
d. Suspended NFA members are viewed as members of the general public and therefore may not transact in futures with the general public while suspended.

6. Which of the following is TRUE of an introducing broker's (IB's) process as it relates to customer funds?

a. They are not responsible for depositing a customer's funds directly into his or her account.
b. Accepting checks made out in his or her own name is not allowed.
c. All funds when deposited go into a "segregated customer funds" account.
d. All of the above are true.

7. Which of the following is NOT a self-regulatory organization (SRO)?

a. National Futures Association (NFA)
b. Commodity Futures Trading Commission (CFTC)
c. Chicago Mercantile Exchange (CME)
d. None of the above

8. The Commodity Futures Trading Commission (CFTC):

I. is a direct government agency.
II. is both appointed and approved by Congress.
III. oversees all futures contracts trading.
IV. is made up of a board of 10 commissioners.

a. I and III
b. I, II, III, and IV
c. II and IV
d. II and III

9. Which of the following is a type of National Futures Association registration available to a firm?

a. Commodity trading advisors
b. Introducing brokers
c. Commodity pool operators
d. All of the above

10. Which of the following is FALSE of the Commodity Exchange Act of 1936?

a. It required that all commodity futures transactions occur on an exchange floor.
b. It was the regulation replacement for the Grain Futures Act of 1922.
c. It allowed for commodity futures options transactions to occur on an exchange floor or in the over-the-counter (OTC) market.
d. It was amended in 1975.

11. A violation of the rules of the Commodity Exchange Act may result in:

I. fines up to $250,000 per violation or the amount of the resulting gain.
II. an individual's registration being revoked.
III. a firm's suspension.
IV. a suspension in trading privileges.

a. I, II, and IV
b. II, III, and IV
c. II only
d. I and III

12. Which of the following is FALSE of a Futures Commission Merchant's (FCM's) clearing process?

a. The FCM chooses the process by which they will clear their trades.
b. Transactions can be cleared on a fully disclosed basis.
c. If trades are cleared on an omnibus basis, the clearing member will know for whom each trade was executed.
d. Customer statements may be sent by the clearing member or the introducing member.

13. The National Futures Association:

I. performs full-scope member audits every 12 months.
II. is a self-regulatory organization (SRO).
III. performs spot audits of members, pre-announced only.
IV. reviews registrations.

a. III and IV
b. I, II, and III
c. I, II, and IV
d. II and IV

14. An AMA commodity pool operator (CPO) is managing two pools, Pool A and Pool B.

	Pool investment	# of investors in pool
Pool A	$325,000	5 investors
Pool B	$175,000	12 investors

Which of the following provides that this CPO be required to register?

a. The total amount of funds invested in Pool A and B together
b. The total number of investors in pools managed by them
c. The amount of funds invested in Pool A
d. The number of investors in Pool B

15. Which of the following regarding a discretionary account is NOT true?

a. Discretionary trades must be approved by the principal on the same day of their execution.
b. Limited power of attorney is required to be signed by the customer for the associated person to have discretionary authority.
c. Even after providing their associated person with discretionary authority over the account, the customer can still enter orders on his or her own behalf.
d. Review of such an account by the principal of the firm is done on a more frequent basis.

16. Advisors must generally register as commodity trading advisors. Which of the following establishes an exception to this rule?

I. The individual is a commodity pool operator.
II. The individual is a floor broker whose primary registered function is not to give such advice.
III. The advisor is an investment club.
IV. The individual is considered by the public to be a commodity trading advisor but has only advised eight clients in the last 12 months.

a. I, II, III, and IV
b. I and IV
c. II and III
d. II, III, and IV

17. Which of the following is TRUE regarding the process of opening a new customer account?

a. A copy of the signed risk disclosure statement is required to be kept only by the futures commission merchant.
b. A commodities risk disclosure statement must be signed by at least one of the parties on the account.
c. A commodities risk disclosure statement must be signed before the account is opened.
d. A commodities account form must be completed and signed by an associated person.

18. A risk disclosure statement must ALWAYS include which of the following?

I. A complete list and description of all account management fees charged by the commodity trading advisor
II. A warning that the document is not necessarily complete in disclosing all risks inherent to the investment
III. A warning that additional inquiry must take place on his or her part regarding redress options available to them in the specific foreign jurisdictions in which their advisor may be engaging in trades
IV. A warning detailing how interacting in foreign markets can result in diminished levels of protection to them as investors than would be provided in the US markets

a. II only
b. I, II, and IV
c. I and II
d. I, III and IV

19. An associated person would like to open and maintain a joint account with another customer. Which of the following is FALSE regarding this process?

a. Confirmations need to be sent only to the associated person in the account.
b. The exchange must be notified of the percentage of participation the associated person has in this joint account.
c. The introducing broker must give permission in writing to the futures commission merchant for the associated person to carry the account.
d. It must be approved by the firm.

20. Which of the following are NOT true of commodity pool operators (CPOs) and their investments?

a. CPOs are required to register if total assets of pool(s) managed is more than $400,000.
b. Investors contribute money into a specific pool and accordingly own a specific interest in only that pool.
c. CPOs are required to register if managing a pool made up of 20 investors or more.
d. CPOs must manage each pool independently.

21. Which of the following are examples of types of account ownership?

I. Corporate
II. Trust
III. Partnership
IV. Individual

a. III and IV
b. I, II, III, and IV
c. I, III, and IV
d. IV only

22. A discretionary account provides the associated person on that account which of the following authorities independent of the client?

a. Amount of contracts to be bought and sold
b. Asset to be bought and sold
c. Determining the action to be taken, whether to buy or sell
d. All of the above

23. The cover page of a risk disclosure document requires which of the following?

I. That it be typed in upper- and lowercase with no caps
II. That it be in boldface type
III. That it include a cautionary statement
IV. That it be positioned specifically as the third page of the document

a. I, II, and III
b. III only
c. I and IV
d. II and III

24. Which of the following is TRUE regarding the process following the death of a customer?

I. Discretionary authority ends immediately.
II. The agent has the authority to proceed forward with instructions given to him or her prior to the customer's death.
III. The agent must liquidate any open futures positions.
IV. The agent must flag the account as "deceased."

a. I and II
b. I, II, III, and IV
c. I, III, and IV
d. III only

25. A commodity trading advisor (CTA) provides advice regarding the values of all of the following EXCEPT

a. swaps.
b. retail off-exchange forex contracts.
c. futures contracts.
d. all of the above.

26. A law firm would like to open an account. Which of the following is TRUE of the partnership agreement?

I. The agreement will indicate who has the authority to enter orders for the account.
II. All members of the firm must receive a copy of the agreement.
III. A resolution must be obtained to determine who will have the authority to enter orders.
IV. It will contain a statement prohibiting the purchase of futures contracts.

a. II and IV
b. I only
c. I, II, III, and IV
d. IV only

27. Which of the following is TRUE regarding a guarantee agreement between an introducing broker and a futures commission merchant?

a. A guarantee agreement warrants that the futures commission merchant may be held civilly liable for the actions of the introducing broker but not criminally liable.
b. A guarantee agreement becomes necessary when the introducing broker cannot maintain $45,000 in minimum net capital.
c. An introducing broker can enter into a guarantee agreement with a maximum of only two futures commission merchants at a time.
d. A guarantee agreement must have a set end date.

28. Associated persons should be proactive in compiling information on their new customers. Which of the following is NOT information normally acquired from the customer?

a. Whether they have futures trading experience
b. A bank reference
c. Their tax returns
d. Their estimated annual income

29. Which of the following is FALSE about a commodity trading advisor?

a. He or she can carry a customer's account.
b. He or she provides trading advice regarding the customer's commodity account.
c. He or she may not accept customer funds.
d. He or she possesses trading authority over a customer's account.

30. Which of the following is NOT true regarding risk disclosure documents?

a. Commodity pool operators are required to file these with the National Futures Association (NFA).
b. Commodity trading advisers are not required to file these with the National Futures Association (NFA).
c. Documents must include a cover page and risk disclosure statement.
d. Documents are to be provided to all prospective investors.

31. Which of the following is TRUE regarding customer account information?

a. A belief that a customer is capable of financially maintaining his or her account can be enough for an associated person to open an account on the customer's behalf.
b. Associated persons are required to make every effort to verify with a third party any information provided to them by the customer.
c. Associated persons may utilize multiple sources when assembling a customer's financial profile.
d. Customers must be willing to provide their financial information to open an account.

32. A commodity pool operator registration exemption exists for operators of commodity investment clubs given which of the following circumstances?

a. The club exists without any advertising provided by the operator.
b. Operation of the club does not provide compensation to the operator.
c. Only one commodity pool is managed at a times
d. All of the above provide an exemption.

33. Which of the following are attributes of a joint tenants in common account?

I. Assets in the account could be distributed unequally.
II. Upon the death of one tenant, all assets go to the surviving party.
III. Both parties on the account share an undivided interest.
IV. One party could have a majority ownership position over the other.

a. II only
b. I, II, and IV
c. I and IV
d. II and III

34. All of the following define a commodity futures trading advisor EXCEPT:

a. Provides advice regarding the trading of futures contracts.
b. Must be an individual, natural person.
c. Receives compensation for services.
d. Provides advice regarding the value of futures contracts.

35. A joint account is defined as one owned by two or more adults. Which of the following is NOT true regarding a joint account?

a. Both parties must sign a commodities risk disclosure document.
b. The associated person on the account must confirm instructions with both parties.
c. The names of all parties on the account should appear on any checks drawn from the account.
d. Both parties on the account can request distributions.

36. Which of the following does NOT need to be included in a risk disclosure statement?

a. A statement regarding the use of leverage and how both losses and gains can be the result of such a strategy
b. A statement detailing how a spread position will always provide less risk than a basic long position
c. A statement explaining how contingent orders will not necessarily limit losses
d. A warning regarding how liquidating a position may be challenging, if not impossible, given the presence of certain market conditions

37. Which of the following can be considered an investment for a commodity pool operator?

I. Options on futures
II. Another commodity pool
III. Retail off-exchange forex contracts
IV. Futures contracts

a. I, II, III, and IV
b. IV only
c. I, III, and IV
d. I and III

38. Which of the following is NOT true of a transfer on a death account?

a. The owner of the account designates in advance who the account will go to in the event of death.
b. In the event the account owner dies, "the beneficiary" will become the new owner.
c. The new owner, with a power of attorney, can enter orders for the account.
d. Should the account owner become the subject of a lawsuit, the account assets will be placed at risk by association.

39. Which of the following is FALSE regarding the National Futures Association's (NFA) business profile questionnaire?

a. If not completed and returned by the member within 60 days of the specified "file by" date, the NFA will view that member as having requested a withdrawal of their NFA membership.
b. It must be completed by the member and submitted on a specified date.
c. It much be sent for completion on an annual basis.
d. It must be sent to member commodity pool operators and commodity trading advisors.

40. Which of the following is TRUE of commodity pool participants?

I. Commodity pool statements are required to show the pool's change in net asset value (NAV) before fees and charges.
II. If the pool is $500,000 or less, participants must receive an annual statement.
III. If the pool is greater than $500,000, participants must receive quarterly statements.
IV. Commodity pool statements must be compiled based on generally accepted accounting principles (GAAP).

a. II and III
b. I, III, and IV
c. IV only
d. I and II

41. Which of the following is NOT true of the discretionary authority on a customer account?

a. Discretionary authority ends when the associated person's employment with the firm ends.
b. Discretion can be transferred from the associated person to another individual as long as that individual is employed by the same firm.
c. A full power of attorney provides authority for cash deposits and withdrawals from the account.
d. Trustees can be granted a full power of attorney.

42. Regarding the rules associated with the management of discretionary accounts, which of the following is FALSE?

a. The account should have a principal who is designated specifically to review that account.
b. If an associated person exercised discretion in a transaction, the order entered must be marked to reflect that.
c. To be granted discretion over a customer's account, an associated person is required to have at least five years of experience.
d. A principal must approve every order by the day after the trade date.

43. Arbitration is a dispute resolution tool. Given that, which of the following is NOT true?

a. Public customers must commit in writing when agreeing to utilize arbitration as their means of dispute resolution.
b. Most claims are regarding financial matters.
c. The customer agreement may contain a dispute arbitration clause.
d. Industry members are offered the option to utilize arbitration in their dispute resolution matters.

44. Under the Patriot Act, anti-money-laundering rules include which of the following?

I. Rules apply to all customers opening an account.
II. The firm's anti-money-laundering program must receive senior management's approval.
III. The firm must implement a customer identification program.
IV. Individuals on the account with only trading authority are not subject to these rules.

a. III only
b. I, II, and III
c. I, III, and IV
d. II and IV

45. Which of the following National Futures Association (NFA) compliance rules requires members to provide their employees with an ethics training program?

a. Rule 4-9
b. Rule 4-2
c. Rule 10-2
d. Rule 2-9

46. Which of the following is TRUE regarding how arbitration dispute cases are handled and resolved?

I. Disputes involving more than $100,000 require three arbitrators.
II. Regardless of the amount of the claim, the number of arbitrators required for a decision must be odd.
III. Disputes of $75,000 or less require only one arbitrator to oversee the case and provide a decision.
IV. A hearing on the claim will allow for the presentation of evidence, but no opportunity for testimony is provided.

a. I, II, and III
b. II, III, and IV
c. I and II
d. III and IV

47. An associated person is accused of money laundering. Which of the following is NOT true regarding their situation?

a. He or she cannot be found guilty if not directly involved in the scheme.
b. He or she can be subject to prosecution.
c. He or she can be fined $500,000 per transaction.
d. He or she can face a potential prison sentence of up to 20 years.

48. Which of the following will be responsible for hearing and determining the outcome of a Commodity Futures Trading Commission (CFTC) hearing?

a. One arbitrator
b. a panel of judges
c. An administrative law judge
d. A panel of three to five arbitrators

49. An aggrieved party, or claimant, files a statement of claim alleging harm caused by another party, the respondent. The amount of the claim is $29,000. How long does this respondent have to respond to this claim?

a. 45 days
b. 28 days
c. 60 days
d. 20 days

50. Members are required to report the receipt of currency from any one customer, in any one day, totaling $10,000 or more, using which of the following forms?

a. 4789
b. 5189
c. 4698
d. 4480

51. In which of the following scenarios is discretionary authority being utilized by the associated person?

I. The associated person determines the best timing for a transaction.
II. The customer specifies the delivery month and year on an order.
III. The customer specifies the number of contracts on the buy order.
IV. The associated person determines the specific commodity on the transaction.

a. IV only
b. I and II
c. I, II, and III
d. III and IV

52. Two parties who are participating in a Commodity Futures Trading Commission proceeding would like to have their decision specifically determined through the submission of papers. Given that, which of the following is the appropriate type of procedure for these two parties?

a. Summary decisional procedure
b. Voluntary decisional procedure
c. Formal decisional procedure
d. Not able to be determined

53. Which of the following are considered steps in the money-laundering process?

I. Purchasing securities into the account
II. Money being deposited into the account
III. Integrating currency back into the banking system
IV. Layering

a. I and III
b. II and III
c. I, II, III, and IV
d. I, II, and IV

54. Which of the following is FALSE of awards resulting from the arbitration process?

a. Those required to pay a monetary award must do so within 30 days of being notified of the decision.
b. Decision notifications are communicated within 30 days.
c. A member's failure to pay an award could result in suspension.
d. All of the above are true.

55. To avoid a possible suspension, which of the following scenarios requires the member to report the receipt of currency?

I. $11,500 from customer D on October 6
II. $3,000 from customer A and $4,500 from customer B on October 1
III. $6,200 from customer A on October 2 and $7,100 from customer A on October 5
IV. $2,500 and $6,800 from customer F on October 10

a. I and III
b. II, III, and IV
c. I only
d. II and IV only

56. Which of the following is FALSE of the guidelines set forth for the National Futures Association ethics training program?

a. It covers when the administration of the program will take place.
b. It covers the ethical obligations owed to the public.
c. It covers how the administration of the program will take place.
d. It covers the topic of how to handle conflicts of interest.

57. An aggrieved party (associated person) would like to file a statement of claim versus a member. What is the maximum amount of time that can pass from this claimant's date of discovery before he or she is prevented from taking any action against this respondent?

a. 6 months
b. 24 months
c. 12 months
d. 36 months

58. Which of the following is TRUE regarding the arbitration process?

a. The claimant must file a submission agreement with the National Futures Association (NFA).
b. Respondents must answer a claim involving $50,000 or more within 60 days.
c. The claimant has a maximum of 2 1/2 years from the date of discovery of a claim to take action.
d. All of the above are true.

59. What does OFAC stand for?

a. Official Foreign Assets Committee
b. Orders for Futures and Commodities
c. Options, Futures, and Commodities
d. Office of Foreign Assets Control

60. Which of the following is TRUE regarding the National Futures Association (NFA) business profile questionnaire?

I. If not submitted within 30 days of receipt, a 30-day grace period will automatically begin for completion.
II. It is sent to designated members every two years.
III. It must be completed and submitted on the specific date provided.
IV. It is sent to NFA members including futures commission merchants and introducing brokers.

a. II and III
b. I and IV
c. III and IV
d. I and II

61. A customer with a claim involving the violation of the Commodities Exchange Act would have to initiate proceedings with which of the following organizations?

a. National Futures Association (NFA)
b. Commodity Futures Trading Commission (CFTC)
c. Futures commission merchants (FCM)
d. Commodity trading advisors (CTA)

62. Which of the following situations could NOT be resolved through arbitration?

a. Customer versus member
b. Member versus associated person
c. Bank versus member
d. All of the above could be solved through arbitration

63. Which of the following are attributes of a summary decisional procedure?

I. A hearing is held only if requested.
II. A decision is expedited and cannot be appealed.
III. The amount in dispute is more than $10,000.
IV. A decision is rendered through the submission of papers.

a. III only
b. I and IV
c. I, II, III, and IV
d. II and IV

64. Changes occurring in reportable positions are communicated to the Commodity Futures Trading Commission through a submission report. Of the following, which is NOT a required change to be reported in this manner?

a. A reported position increase
b. A decrease in a reported position
c. All positions as they are opened
d. The close of a reported position

65. Which of the following is TRUE of a buy limit order?

a. The order must be executed once entered; cancellation is not an option.
b. The investor is provided control over the price he or she pays for contracts.
c. It guarantees the maximum price to be paid by the investor and that the order will be executed.
d. All of the above are true

66. A customer has an order in futures contracts executed in his or her account on a Monday. He or she is sent a transaction confirmation on Wednesday. The confirmation contains the customer and futures commission merchant's (FCM) name as well as the account number. It also shows the trade date but not settlement date, price, amount due, or whether it is a covered or uncovered option. Which of the following details regarding this transaction goes against what is required by industry rules?

I. No settlement date on the confirmation.
II. The transaction confirmation not including the amount due
III. The day the customer received the transaction confirmation
IV. The FCM's name on the confirmation

a. I and IV
b. III only
c. II and IV
d. I, II, and III

67. Which of the following are FALSE of "not held orders"?

a. They are also known as "disregard tape orders."
b. The floor broker has discretion regarding the timing of the execution.
c. The investor retains discretion over the price of execution.
d. They are day orders unless received in writing and entered good till cancelled (GTC).

68. An investor purchased 2 September wheat futures contracts at 8.65. The contract is trending up in price, peaking at 11.35. The investor, going forward, would like to sell the contracts and maximize his or her profit but is concerned that the price will start trading lower, possibly reaching 9.00. Which of the following orders should he or she enter to protect and maximize profit?

a. Buy 2 September wheat futures at 8.00 stop.
b. Sell 2 September wheat futures at 10.25 stop.
c. Sell 2 September wheat futures at 8.25 stop.
d. Sell 2 September wheat futures at 9.45 stop.

69. Which of the following is TRUE regarding the National Futures Association's (NFA) investigation of alleged violations and complaints?

I. Members may be subject to an unannounced onsite review performed by the NFA.
II. Full NFA member audits are conducted every 36 months.
III. All complaints originate from the NFA.
IV. All NFA complaints are treated equally in terms of merit and worthiness of investigation.

a. II and IV
b. I only
c. III and IV
d. I, II, and III

70. An investor is long 7 April corn futures contracts at a basis of 12.50. At which of the following prices will this investor be able to sell his or her 7 April corn futures contracts while maximizing the profit on the transaction?

a. 12.00
b. 13.25
c. 12.25
d. 13.75

71. How would an investor wanting to purchase crude oil enter a limit order for 6 September contracts at a maximum price of $2.15?

a. Buy 6 September crude oil @2.15 stop.
b. Buy 6 September crude oil MKT.
c. Buy 6 September crude oil @2.15.
d. None of the above is correct.

72. A member having violated a National Futures Association's (NFA) rule will potentially face which of the following penalties?

I. Automatic membership expulsion
II. Restitution
III. A total maximum fine of $250,000
IV. Censured

a. II and IV
b. I, III, and IV
c. I, II, III, and IV
d. I and III

73. An investor who wants to create an order that will stay open without expiring each day would open what kind of order?

a. Market/day order.
b. Fill-or-kill (FOK) order.
c. Good-til-cancelled (GTC) order.
d. One-cancels-the-other (OCTO) order.

74. Which of the following are FALSE of customer account statements?

a. Customers must receive account statements for every month they have activity in their accounts.
b. A customer who has not had activity on an account must receive an account statement at least biannually.
c. Account statements must include credit and debit balances.
d. Examples of "account activity" would include interest received.

75. Which of the following is FALSE of "all or none orders"?

a. They are not displayed in the market.
b. They may be entered as day orders.
c. They may be entered as "good till cancel" (GTC).
d. All of the above are true.

76. Which of the following is NOT considered a "live order"?

a. Stop order
b. Market order
c. Sell limit order
d. Buy limit order

77. Regarding member reasonability actions, which of the following statements is FALSE?

a. They could result in the violating member ceasing to do business.
b. The president of the National Futures Association (NFA) must be in agreement with the board of directors to initiate this action.
c. An action can proceed with or without a hearing.
d. All of the above are true.

78. Which of the following is TRUE of a market order?

I. Will be filled at the best available price as soon as possible.
II. An investor can place a limit on the maximum price he or she will pay.
III. It gives the investor the greatest chance of having their order filled.
IV. It is best utilized by an investor looking to limit or guard against a loss.

a. I and III
b. I only
c. II and IV
d. II, III, and IV

79. Which of the following is TRUE regarding record keeping for customer accounts?

a. Futures commission merchants (FCM) must handle all record keeping, including account confirmations and statements, for each of their accounts.
b. In the event an introducing broker (IB) is involved, he or she is also required to maintain all of the appropriate records on customer accounts.
c. Both FCMs and IBs can maintain orders in a daily journal, but only FCMs are required to do so.
d. Requirements for record keeping apply only to accounts of customers who are transacting business directly with an FCM.

80. Which of the following is FALSE of a limit order?

a. A sell limit order provides the investor the opportunity to set the minimum price he or she will accept in the sale of a futures contract.
b. A sell limit order does not have guaranteed execution.
c. Limit orders can sometimes be referred to as "resting orders."
d. Futures contracts trading at an investor's limit price will guarantee that the order was executed.

81. Communications are defined as which of the following?

I. Hypothetical calculations are never allowed
II. Opinions that must be clearly stated as such
III. Only those distributed via hard-copy form
IV. Written communications members must retain for three years from the date when they last used them

a. I, II, and IV
b. II only
c. I and II
d. III and IV

82. An investor establishes a short position by selling 5 May silver futures contracts at 67.25. If the investor buys to close the position at 65.75, what is the total gain/loss on the order?

a. $75 loss.
b. $75 gain.
c. $750 gain.
d. $750 loss.

83. Which of the following is the correct way to enter a limit on an open market order to buy 5 April wheat contracts with the price limit of 32.50 or better to be executed during the opening range of the market?

a. Buy 5 April wheat at 32.50 market on open.
b. Buy 5 April wheat market opening only.
c. Buy 5 April wheat at open 32.50.
d. Buy 5 April wheat at 32.50 opening only.

84. Which of the following would NOT be considered a benefit to utilizing futures contracts?

a. Opportunities to obtain credit at higher rates
b. Reduction in commodity cost
c. Lower prices on finished goods
d. Reduced buyer and seller concerns over large price swings in the market

85. Which of the following is NOT a type of order?

a. Exchange for physical order
b. Market if exchanged
c. Give up order
d. Bunched order

86. Which of the following is TRUE of delivery months for commodity futures contracts?

I. Futures contracts can trade with delivery in all 12 calendar months.
II. Futures contracts are listed with the more distant delivery months listed first.
III. They are set by exchanges on which the futures contract trades.
IV. Futures contracts are listed by both commodity and delivery month.

a. I and II
b. I and IV
c. III and IV
d. II and III

87. Which of the following is NOT accurate of a "limit or market on close" order to buy seven September crude contracts at a price of 8.50 or better?

a. The order could be entered as "Buy seven September crude market on close or 8.50."
b. The investor can initially designate the order be executed at a limit price or better.
c. It provides for flexibility in execution of the order.
d. The investor stipulates a guaranteed execution of this order during that trading session.

88. Which of the following is described as the minimum amount of margin required for continuing to hold a position?

a. Original maintenance margin
b. Minimum maintenance margin
c. Minimum floor margin
d. None of the above

89. Which of the following is TRUE of a "market if touched" order?

a. The order to sell would strategically be entered above the market.
b. It becomes a market order to buy or sell at the next available price.
c. It is also known as a "board order."
d. All of the above are true.

90. Which of the following is TRUE of forward contracts?

I. The buyer always has option to decline delivery.
II. They are privately negotiated contracts.
III. Having a third individual take over the contractual obligation of one of the original two parties in the event that one of them fails to perform is prohibited.
IV. The seller is always obligated to deliver on contract.

a. I, II, III
b. II and IV
c. II only
d. I and III

91. Which of the following orders involves an investor either buying or selling futures contracts at specific intervals?

a. Basis order
b. Scale order
c. Give up order
d. Bunched order

92. Which of the following is used as a proxy for the opening price of the market in the United States day by day?

a. Beta inversions.
b. T-Bill rates.
c. Market short interest.
d. S&P 500 futures.

93. Which of the following are TRUE of trading futures on an exchange floor?

I. Firms are exempt from requirements held for individuals to trade on an exchange floor.
II. Trading practices are regulated by the exchange itself.
III. Individuals are required to own a membership to trade.
IV. Buyers and sellers establish the margin requirements for their contracts.

a. I and III
b. II and IV
c. II and III
d. I and IV

94. Which of the following is NOT true of a forward contract?

a. It can be obtained in a secondary market.
b. It is utilized by banks doing international business.
c. Counterparty risk is inherent in the transaction.
d. No entity exists to enforce the contract or compensate for the default of the obligation.

95. Which of the following is a properly entered "cancels former order" (CFO)?

a. Buy 9 April wheat at 8.25 CFO
b. Buy 9 April wheat CFO at 8.25
c. CFO Buy 9 April wheat at 8.25
d. CFO Buy 9 April 8.25 wheat

96. The futures exchange provides both producers and users the opportunity to do all of the following EXCEPT

a. hedge risk.
b. negotiate contract specifics.
c. lock in prices for commodities.
d. manage aspects of their business.

97. Which of the following describes a "market on open" order?

I. There can be no partial executions on these types of orders.
II. The order will be cancelled if not executed at the opening of the market.
III. "Opening of market" is considered immediately upon the open, not a range of time after the opening.
IV. Limit orders are allowed.

a. II and IV
b. I and II
c. I, II, III, and IV
d. IV only

98. Which of the following is FALSE of futures contracts?

I. Contract terms and conditions are negotiated specifically between the parties of the contract.
II. They can be utilized in the trading of Treasury securities.
III. It is a contract involving two parties.
IV. They are not traded in a secondary market.

a. I, II, and IV
b. I and III
c. II only
d. I and IV

99. An investor buys nine May corn contracts at a price of 2.25. He or she would like to sell their corn contracts higher to realize a profit but also seeks a strategy that will protect from suffering a loss on this position. Which of the following types of orders would BEST provide the strategy he or she is seeking?

a. Cancels former order (CFO)
b. One order cancels the other (OCO)
c. All or none order
d. Market if touched (MIT)

100. Which of the following is FALSE of a bunched order?

a. Allocation of the order must be accomplished within 24 hours of the order's execution.
b. It involves one single order.
c. Allocation of the futures contracts can occur after the order's execution.
d. It is executed for the accounts of several different clients.

101. Which of the following are examples of being long or short the commodity?

I. A cattle farmer needs corn to feed cattle and does not grow the corn himself; he or she is "short" the corn commodity.
II. A producer has 290 barrels of oil; he or she is "long" 200 barrels of oil.
III. A commodity producer has the commodity immediately on hand; he or she is "long" the commodity.
IV. An individual is under contract to deliver some amount of wheat but does not currently own wheat in that amount; he or she is "short" the wheat commodity.

a. I and III
b. I, II, III, and IV
c. II and IV
d. III only

102. An investor would like to enter a "cancels former order" (CFO) order. Which of the following are examples of changes he or she may make to the original existing order in doing so?

a. Changing day order to a "good till cancel" (GTC) order
b. Number of contracts
c. Limiting price
d. All of the above

103. When comparing forward contracts versus futures contracts, which of the following is TRUE of a futures contract?

I. Liquid secondary market
II. Counterparty risk
III. Performance guarantees
IV. Standardized contracts

a. II and III
b. IV only
c. I, III, and IV
d. I and II

104. Which of the following is TRUE of a floor trader?

a. He or she may take on long-term positions.
b. In the absence of any buy or sell orders to execute, he or she can opt not to execute orders.
c. He or she may participate in day trading.
d. All of the above are true.

105. Which of the following is FALSE of the commodity delivery process?

I. Delivery can be made directly to the buyer if all parties agree.
II. If multiple approved delivery locations are available, the buyer will decide to which location he or she will accept delivery.
III. The delivery process is determined by the exchange within which the commodity contract trades.
IV. Once delivery has been made, the buyer can request to have it inspected for quality grade and quantity.

a. I, II, and IV
b. I and III.
c. III only
d. II only

106. Which of the following is FALSE of a commodity futures option?

a. It is a contract between two parties.
b. The buyer pays for the right to buy or sell the contract.
c. The seller is provided the "option" to perform under the contract.
d. The buyer pays a premium.

107. If a large institution begins to buy up the entire supply of any given commodity, they are said to be:

a. Frontrunning.
b. Cornering the market.
c. Marking to market.
d. Stabilizing.

108. Which of the following are indicative of a "bearish" outlook?

I. Buys call with the belief that the price of the futures contract will rise.
II. Sells put with the belief that the price of the futures contract will rise.
III. Buys put with belief that the price of the futures contract will fall.
IV. Sells call with belief that the price of the futures contract will fall.

a. III and IV
b. I and II
c. I and III
d. II and IV

109. A buyer determining whether to establish a position in commodity futures should consider all of the following EXCEPT

a. the breakeven scenario for the transaction.
b. the maximum gain in the transaction.
c. the amount of premium he or she will be paid for the transaction.
d. the maximum loss in the transaction.

110. Which of the following is FALSE regarding an investor who purchases a futures contract put?

a. He or she believes the futures contract price will decrease.
b. The maximum gain equals contract strike price minus the premium.
c. He or she looks for limited maximum gain.
d. All of the above are true.

111. An investor is short 1 September wheat 700 call at 4. What will be the maximum gain, maximum loss, and breakeven on this position?

a. The maximum gain is $4, maximum loss is unlimited, and breakeven is $700.
b. The maximum gain is unlimited, maximum loss is $400, and breakeven is $704.
c. The maximum gain is $400, maximum loss is unlimited, and breakeven is $704.
d. The maximum gain is $400, maximum loss is unlimited, and breakeven is $700.

112. Cash corn is trading at $6.16 per bushel. There's a monthly storage fee of $.10 per bushel and a monthly insurance cost per bushel of $.02. Given these parameters, what would be the total cost per bushel to buy the corn and hold onto it for four months?

a. $6.28
b. $6.16
c. $6.40
d. $6.64

113. An investor is "long 1 March corn 75 call at 2." What will the maximum gain and breakeven be on this position?

a. Unlimited gain, $77 breakeven
b. $20 gain, $77 breakeven
c. Unlimited gain, $73 breakeven
d. $2 gain, $73 breakeven

114. Which of the following is FALSE of the clearinghouse process?

a. Members must deposit the required margin, as calculated by the clearinghouse, by the next trading day's open.
b. Members will report all transactions to the clearinghouse.
c. Futures contract trades settle the same business day.
d. All of the above are true.

115. Which of the following is TRUE of an option seller?

I. He or she is obligated to perform under contract.
II. His or her main objective is for premium income.
III. He or she is known as the "writer."
IV. His or her goal is to have the option expire without being exercised.

a. II and IV
b. I, II, III, and IV
c. I and III
d. I only

116. Which of the following is NOT a reason investors might choose to purchase call options on futures contracts?

a. A user hedges against a price decrease for a commodity.
b. Lacking the funds to purchase the contracts immediately, the investor seeks to lock in a purchase price for a futures contract with the commodity to be delivered at a future date when they will possess the funds.
c. The investor profits from price appreciation on the futures contract.
d. All of the above are reasons investors might purchase call options.

117. Options are classified as to which of the following?

a. Class
b. Type
c. Series
d. All of the above

118. Which of the following is FALSE of trading futures contracts?

a. They may be traded in the over-the-counter (OTC) market.
b. Disputes are resolved by the exchange's floor committee.
c. All trades occur in the pits.
d. Trades are reported to the tape so as to be communicated to the marketplace.

119. When considering a futures call option position's maximum gain or loss, which of the following is FALSE?

a. Profit occurs from a rise in the price of the futures contract.
b. Maximum loss is not limited to the premium paid for the option.
c. Maximum gain will be similar to if a futures contract has been purchased.
d. Maximum gain is unlimited.

120. Which of the following is FALSE regarding maximum gain, loss, and breakeven for call buyers versus call sellers?

I. The call seller's maximum loss is unlimited.
II. The buyer and seller will break even at the same point.
III. The buyer's maximum gain is the seller's maximum loss.
IV. The call buyer's maximum loss is unlimited.

a. IV only
b. I and III
c. II and III
d. I, II, and IV

Answer Key and Explanations

1. B: An introducing broker is defined as an organization that solicits orders for customers in the futures market. A commodity pool operator is an organization that is responsible for the investment of funds contributed specifically by a group of participants into one single account and into, among other things, futures contracts. A futures commission merchant is a firm that executes futures orders for its customers' accounts.

2. A: Individuals working within the futures industry in supervisory roles are required to seek National Futures Association (NFA) registration as an associated person. Individuals seeking registration however must NOT file an application directly with the NFA through the Online Registration System (ORS) and instead should request that their firm file the application for them. Firms doing business within the futures industry are required to register with the NFA, and an individuals' assigned NFA ID numbers will NOT change throughout their career in the futures industry.

3. D: The Commodity Futures Trading Commission (CFTC) in having authoritative jurisdiction over all commodity exchanges and its participating floor brokers will monitor exchange activity for signs of price manipulation, approve the terms of all futures and options contracts, and can seek a restraining order against someone found in violation of the rules. Under no circumstances can an employee of the CFTC trade futures contracts.

4. A: A Futures Commission Merchant (FCM) executes orders for customer accounts and is required to file monthly statements of financial condition. They are also required to maintain a minimum net capital of at least $1 million, NOT $1.5 million. They may be a member of the clearing corporation, but only if they maintain their customers' accounts, and are responsible for holding their cash and securities.

5. C: To transact in futures with the general public, National Futures Association (NFA) membership is required. NFA member transactions are limited to only those involving other NFA members; suspended NFA members are viewed as members of the general public and therefore may not transact in futures with the general public while suspended. NFA members can however share commissions.

6. D: An introducing broker is not responsible for depositing customer funds directly into an account, but instead the funds are deposited by a futures commission merchant. All funds are deposited on the day of receipt into a "segregated customer funds" account, and accepting checks made out in their own name is strictly forbidden.

7. B: A self-regulatory organization (SRO) is defined as an organization that has the authority to regulate its own members. Two examples of this are the National Futures Association (NFA) and the Chicago Mercantile Exchange (CME). The Commodity Futures Trading Commission (CFTC) is NOT an SRO.

8. A: The Commodity Futures Trading Commission (CFTC) is a direct government agency overseeing all futures contracts trading. It is made up of five commissioners, NOT 10; these commissioners are appointed by the president and only approved by Congress.

9. D: Firms, depending on the type of business they conduct, may seek National Futures Association registration as commodity trading advisors (CTA), introducing brokers (IB), or commodity pool operators (CPO).

10. C: The Commodity Exchange Act of 1936 was the regulation replacement for the Grain Futures Act of 1922 and required that all commodity futures transactions occur on an exchange floor; it was amended in 1975. It did allow for commodity futures options transactions to occur on an exchange floor but did NOT allow for them to occur in the over the counter (OTC) market.

11. B: A violation of the rules of the Commodity Exchange Act may result in an individual's registration being revoked, a firm's suspension, or a suspension in trading privileges. Fines may be imposed for such violations but up to a maximum of $140,000 per violation, NOT $250,000, or three times the amount of the resulting gain, NOT simply the amount of the gain itself.

12. C: A futures commission merchant (FCM) chooses the process by which he or she will clear trades. Transactions can be cleared on a fully disclosed basis, and if so, all customer statements and confirmations will be sent by the clearing member. If the FCM chooses to clear trades on an omnibus basis, the clearing member will NOT know for whom each trade was executed, and the introducing member will be responsible for sending all customer confirmations and statements.

13. D: The National Futures Association is a self-regulatory organization (SRO) whose responsibilities include reviewing registrations. They also perform full-scope member audits every 24 months, NOT every 12, and perform unannounced spot audits of members.

14. A: This commodity pool operator (CPO) would be required to register as a CPO because of the total amount of funds invested in Pool A and B together, which is $500,000. Registration is required when the total assets of all pools managed by the CPO is more than $400,000. A CPO could also be required to register given that he or she manages an individual pool with 15 or more investors. Here, Pool A had only five investors, and Pool B had 12.

15. A: Discretionary trades are required to be approved by the principal of the firm within one day of their execution, NOT the same day. Review of such an account by the principal of the firm is done on a frequent basis. A limited power of attorney is required to be signed by the customer for the associated person to have discretionary authority, and even after providing the associated person with discretionary authority over the account, the customer can still enter orders on his or her own behalf.

16. C: Advisors must generally register as commodity trading advisors. Exceptions to this rule include when the individual is a floor broker whose primary registered function is not to give such advice and when the advisor is an investment club. The individual who is a commodity pool operator would NOT be exempt from registration. The individual who has advised only eight clients over the last 12 months would only be exempt if he or she had not already publicly represented him- or herself as being a commodity trading advisor.

17. D: To open an account for a new customer, a commodities account form must be completed and signed by an associated person. A commodities risk disclosure statement must be signed at the time of or before the opening of the new account. The commodities risk disclosure statement must be signed by all parties to the account, NOT only one. A copy of the signed risk disclosure statement is required to be kept by both the introducing broker and the futures commission merchant.

18. C: A risk disclosure statement must always include a complete list and description of all account management fees charged by the commodity trading advisor and a warning that the document is not necessarily complete in disclosing al risks inherent to the investment. Only if this commodity trading advisor trades in foreign futures, or options contracts on foreign exchanges will it be necessary to include a warning that additional inquiry must take place on his or her part regarding redress options available in the specific foreign jurisdictions in which the advisor may be engaging in trades and a warning detailing how interacting in foreign markets can result in diminished levels of protection as investors than would be provided in the US markets.

19. A: An associated person would like to open and maintain a joint account with another customer. Before the account can be opened, it must first be approved by the firm. The exchange must be notified of the percentage of participation the associated person has in this joint account, and the introducing broker must give permission in writing to the futures commission merchant for them to carry the account. Confirmations, however, must be sent to the customer with whom the associated person has the joint account.

20. C: Investors, when contributing to a commodity pool, are investing into a specific pool and accordingly own a specific interest in only that pool. Commodity pool operators (CPOs) must manage each pool independently and are required to register if the total assets of the pool(s) they manage is more than $400,000. They are also required to register if they manage a pool made up of 15 investors or more, NOT 20.

21. B: There are five types of account ownership. They are corporate, trust, partnership, individual, and joint.

22. D: A discretionary account provides the associated person on that account the authority to determine, independent of their client, the amount of contracts to be bought and sold, the asset to be bought and sold, and the action to be taken on the account—whether to buy or sell.

23. D: The cover page of a risk disclosure document is required to be typed in boldface and to include a cautionary statement. It does NOT have to be typed in upper- and lowercase and, in fact, is required to be in all caps. Further, there is no requirement that it be positioned specifically as the third page of the document.

24. C: Following the death of a customer, the agent must flag the account as "deceased" and liquidate any open futures positions. If the account is discretionary, discretionary authority would immediately cease on that account. Further, the agent must NOT proceed with instructions given prior to the customer's death and instead must wait on instructions given by whoever is the administrator of the estate.

25. D: A commodity trading advisor (CTA) provides advice regarding the values of swaps, retail off-exchange forex contracts, and futures contracts.

26. B: A partnership agreement for a law firm would indicate who has the authority to enter orders for the account. All members of the firm do NOT receive a copy of the agreement; only the associated person related to the account is required. Unlike for a corporate account, a resolution is NOT required to determine who will have the authority to enter orders. The agreement cannot prohibit the purchase of futures contracts.

27. B: A guarantee agreement becomes necessary when the introducing broker cannot maintain $45,000 in minimum net capital. The futures commission merchant is then acting to guarantee the introducing broker's solvency. A guarantee agreement does warrant that the futures commission merchant may be held civilly liable for the actions of the introducing broker, but he or she may also be held criminally liable too. An introducing broker may only enter into a guarantee agreement with one futures commission merchant at a time, NOT two, and the agreement itself can be held open-ended if necessary, with no set end date stated up front.

28. C: Associated persons in compiling information on their new customers might request a bank reference, their estimated annual income, and whether they have futures trading experience. They will NOT go as far as to request their tax returns.

29. A: A commodity trading advisor provides trading advice regarding his or her customer's commodity account and possesses trading authority over the customer's account. He or she does not have the authority to accept customer funds. Additionally, he or she may NOT carry a customer's account. Instead, customer accounts must be carried at a futures commission merchant.

30. B: Both commodity pool operators and commodity trading advisors are required to file risk disclosure documents with the National Futures Association (NFA). The documents must include a cover page and risk disclosure statement and, once filed with the NFA, are to be provided to all prospective investors.

31. A: A belief that a customer is capable of financially maintaining his or her account can be enough for an associated person to open an account on the customer's behalf. Given that the customer information provided came directly from the customer, the associated person is NOT required to make every effort to verify with a third party any information provided by the customer. When assembling a customer's financial profile, the customer should be the sole source of information. Customers are NOT required to disclose all financial information to open an account.

32. D: A commodity pool operator registration exemption exists for operators of commodity investment clubs given that the club exists without any advertising provided by the operator, the operation of the club does not provide compensation to the operator, and only one commodity pool is managed at a time by the operator.

33. C: In a joint tenants in common account, assets in the account could be distributed unequally, and one party could have a majority ownership position over the other. The parties in the account do NOT share an undivided interest, and upon the death of one tenant, all assets go to the decedent's estate, NOT to the surviving party to the account.

34. B: A commodity trading advisor can be an individual or a business. They receive compensation for services, provide advice regarding the trading of futures contracts, and provide advice regarding the value of futures contracts.

35. B: The associated person on a joint account is NOT required to confirm instructions with both parties on the account. Both parties on the account must sign a commodities risk disclosure document, both parties can request distributions, and the names of all parties on the account should appear on any checks drawn from the account.

36. B: A risk disclosure statement should include a statement regarding the use of leverage and how both losses and gains can be the result of such a strategy, a statement explaining how contingent orders will not necessarily limit losses, and a warning regarding how liquidating a position may be challenging, if not impossible, given the presence of certain market conditions. There is however no statement detailing how a spread position will always provide less risk than a basic long position given that it could in fact provide more.

37. A: Commodity pool operators make investments through a single account on behalf of a group of investors. Potentially they may invest in options on futures, retail off-exchange forex contracts, futures contracts, or another commodity pool.

38. D: A transfer on death account provides for the owner of the account to designate in advance who the account will go to in the event of death. Should a transfer on death account owner die, "the beneficiary" will become the new owner. That new owner, with a power of attorney, can enter orders for the account. Should the account owner become the subject of a lawsuit, the account assets will NOT be placed at risk by association, as is the case with a joint tenants with rights of survivorship account.

39. A: The National Futures Association (NFA) sends a business profile questionnaire on an annual basis to member commodity pool operators and commodity trading advisors. It must be completed by the member and submitted on a specified date. If the member fails to complete and return the questionnaire within 30, NOT 60 days, of the specified "file by" date, the NFA will view that member as having requested a withdrawal of NFA membership.

40. C: Commodity pool statements must be compiled based on generally accepted accounting principles (GAAP). If the commodity pool is greater than $500,000, participants must receive monthly statements, NOT quarterly, and if the pool is $500,000 or less, participants must receive quarterly statements, NOT an annual statement. Last, commodity pool statements are required to show the pool's change in net asset value (NAV), including fees and charges.

41. B: Discretionary authority cannot be transferred to another individual under any circumstances and will end when the associated person's employment with the firm ends. A full power of attorney provides authority for cash deposits and withdrawals from an account, and an example of an individual customarily granted a full power of attorney is a trustee.

42. C: To be granted discretion over a customer's account, an associated person is required to have at least two years of experience, NOT five. The account should have a principal who is designated specifically to review that account, the principal must approve every order by the day after the trade date, and if an associated person exercised discretion in a transaction, the order entered must be marked to reflect that.

43. D: Industry members are required to utilize arbitration in their dispute resolution matters; it is NOT optional. Most arbitration claims are regarding financial matters. Public customers must commit in writing when agreeing to utilize arbitration as their means of dispute resolution, and the customer agreement may contain the dispute arbitration clause.

44. B: Under the Patriot Act, a firm's anti-money-laundering program must receive its senior management's approval, a firm must implement a customer identification program, and anti-money-laundering rules apply to all customers who open an account. Individuals on the account with only trading authority however are subject to these rules as well.

45. D: The National Futures Association (NFA) compliance Rule 2-9 requires members to provide their employees with an ethics training program.

46. C: Disputes involving more than $100,000 require three arbitrators, and it is true that regardless of the amount of the claim, the number of arbitrators required for a decision must always be odd. Only one arbitrator is required for disputes of $50,000 or less, NOT $75,000. A hearing on the claim will allow for the presentation of both evidence and testimony.

47. A: An associated person who is accused of money laundering can be found guilty even in the absence of being directly involved in the scheme. He or she could also be subject to prosecution and face a fine of $500,000 per transaction and/or a potential prison sentence of up to 20 years.

48. C: An administrative law judge will be responsible for hearing and determining the outcome of a Commodity Futures Trading Commission (CFTC) hearing.

49. D: This respondent has a maximum of 20 days to respond to this statement of claim. That is the maximum amount of time given a respondent for a claim against them of less than $50,000.

50. A: Members are required to report the receipt of currency from any one customer, in any one day, totaling $10,000 or more, using a currency transaction report, or form 4789.

51. A: Discretionary authority is utilized in the scenario involving the associated person determining the specific commodity on the transaction. An associated person can independently determine the best timing for a transaction without having a written power of attorney, and so accordingly it would not qualify as utilizing discretionary authority. Discretionary authority is not utilized in scenarios involving a customer specifying either the delivery month and year on an order or the number of contracts on the buy order.

52. A: Two parties who are participating in a Commodity Futures Trading Commission proceeding and who would like to have their decision specifically determined through the submission of papers would be best served to proceed with a summary decisional procedure. A voluntary decisional procedure would entail the participation of a judgment officer, and a formal decisional procedure would be resolved through a formal hearing.

53. C: The money-laundering process starts with money being deposited into the account. "Layering" involves making a variety of deposits into the account, all being in amounts that are less than $10,000. Next will be to purchase securities into the account, thus integrating currency back into the banking system.

54. D: Award notifications that result from arbitration are communicated within 30 days, those required to pay a monetary award must do so within 30 days of their being notified of the decision, and a member's failure to pay an award could result in suspension.

55. C: Members are required to report the receipt of currency in the amount of $10,000 or more from any one customer in any one day. Further, they must report multiple deposits made from a single customer in one day totaling $10,000 or more. The receipt of $11,500 from customer D on October 6 is the only scenario in this question that would require a report due to it being in an amount that is more than $10,000 and from one customer in one day.

56. A: The guidelines set forth for the National Futures Association ethics training program include how the administration of the program will take place but NOT when the administration of the program will take place. It also covers topics regarding ethical obligations owed to the public and how to handle conflicts of interest.

57. B: An aggrieved party (associated person) who would like to file a statement of claim versus a member has up to two years, or 24 months, from the claim's date of discovery before they are prevented from taking any action against the respondent.

58. A: A claimant must file a submission agreement with the National Futures Association (NFA). He or she has a maximum of two years, NOT two and a half, from the date of discovery of the claim to take action, and the respondent must answer a claim involving $50,000 or more within 45 days, NOT 60.

59. D: OFAC stands for the Office of Foreign Assets Control, a suborganization of the Treasury Department. They maintain a list of suspected terrorists and criminals that firms must utilize as a reference for their customers. Business conducted with anyone on this list is strictly prohibited.

60. C: The National Futures Association (NFA) business profile questionnaire is sent to NFA members, including futures commission merchants and introducing brokers, and must be completed and submitted on the specific date provided. It is however sent to designated members on an annual basis, NOT every two years. It must also be filed upon completion within 30 days of the specified return date. A failure to do so will communicate to the NFA the desire to withdraw membership, and a notification of such a status will immediately be sent to the member.

61. B: A customer with a claim involving the violation of the Commodities Exchange Act would have to initiate proceedings with the Commodity Futures Trading Commission (CFTC). The National Futures Association (NFA) oversees the futures industry as a whole, focusing on ethical behavior, training, and member audits. Futures commission merchants (FCMs) transact in futures, including executing customer orders. A Commodity trading advisor (CTA) acts as a paid advisor to others in the area of trading futures contracts and/or futures contracts options.

62. D: The types of matters that could be resolved through arbitration include customer versus member, member versus associated person, and bank versus member.

63. B: A summary decisional procedure involves a decision being rendered through the submission of papers and a hearing being held only by request. A voluntary decisional procedure provides for a decision that is expedited and one that cannot be appealed. A formal decisional procedure is appropriate for a disputed amount greater than $10,000.

64. C: It is NOT necessary to report all positions as they are opened via a submission report. The only changes in reportable positions that are required to be communicated are a reported position increase, a decrease in a reported position, and the close of a reported position.

65. B: A buy limit order provides the investor with the opportunity to set a maximum price for a futures contract he or she would like to purchase. Accordingly, this allows them to have some control over the price he or she will ultimately pay for the contracts. The maximum price paid by the investor will be guaranteed but the execution will NOT be. The order once entered may NOT be executed if the futures contract does not trade down to the maximum price set by the investor.

66. D: Industry rules dictate that trade confirmations resulting from an order in futures contracts must include both the trade settlement date and the amount due. Also, the trade confirmation must be sent to the customer by the business day immediately after the transaction date, NOT two days after. The name of the futures commission merchant (FCM) is also required and was included here in this example.

67. C: "Not held orders" are also known as "disregard tape orders." They are considered day orders unless received in writing and entered good till cancelled (GTC), and the floor broker will have discretion regarding the timing of the execution of these orders. The investor does NOT retain discretion over the price of execution; the floor broker does.

68. B: An investor having purchased 2 September wheat futures contracts at 8.65 would like to protect and maximize the profit given his or her desire to sell sometime in the near future. The contracts are trading at a high of 11.35, but the investor believes that the price will begin to drop, possibly to as low as 9.00. The order he or she should enter to protect and maximize those profits is "sell 2 September wheat futures at 10.25 stop." If these contracts trade down to or through 10.25, a market order will be triggered to sell at that price, thus providing a profit for that investor. A "sell 2 September wheat futures at 9.45 stop" order will provide profit but less than the order to sell at 10.25. A "sell 2 September wheat futures at 8.25 stop" will NOT provide any profit given the 8.25 sell price is below the purchase price of 8.65.

69. B: The National Futures Association (NFA), in investigating alleged violations and complaints, may perform unannounced onsite reviews of members. All complaints however, do NOT originate with NFA staff; some may originate from customers of member firms or other members. Once the NFA receives a complaint, it is then determined whether it has the merit to be investigated; NOT all complaints are found to have merit. Full member audits are conducted every 24 months, NOT every 36.

70. D: An investor who purchased 7 April corn futures contracts at 12.50 would maximize profits here by selling at 13.75. Selling at 13.25 would provide some profit but less than 13.75, and selling at either 12.00 or 12.25 would produce a loss, having purchased the contracts at 12.50.

71. C: An investor wanting to enter a limit order to purchase 6 crude oil September contracts at a maximum price of $2.15 would enter "Buy 6 September crude oil @2.15." Entering "Buy 6 September crude oil @2.15 stop" would be appropriate for a buy stop order, and entering "Buy 6 September crude oil MKT" would be appropriate for a market order.

72. A: A member, having violated a National Futures Association (NFA) rule, will potentially face the penalties of restitution and censure. He or she may face a fine, but it will be $250,000 per violation, NOT a maximum total fine of $250,000. He or she may also be expelled from membership, but imposition of that penalty requires a two-thirds vote; it is NOT automatic.

73. C: "GTC" for an order stands for "good till cancel." This is an order where the investor has the ability to designate that the order remain active until it is cancelled. This is different than a day order, which is cancelled at the end of the trading day if not executed.

74. B: A customer who has not had activity on his or her account must receive an account statement at least quarterly, NOT biannually. Customers must receive account statements for every month they have activity in their account, and account statements must include credit and debit balances. Examples of "account activity" would include interest received.

75. D: "All or none orders" are not displayed in the market and may be entered as day orders or as "good till cancel" (GTC) orders.

76. A: Stop orders are NOT considered to be "live orders." This type of order must be "elected" to be used. This occurs when the futures contract trades at or through the stop or trigger price, at which time it becomes a market order. A market order has guaranteed execution at the time it is presented to the market, and limit orders are triggered once the limit price is reached.

77. D: The president of the National Futures Association (NFA) must be in agreement with the board of directors to initiate this action; this action can proceed with or without a hearing, and the result of this action may be that the violating member is forced to cease doing business.

78. A: The execution of a market order is more likely than the execution of a limit or stop order. Market orders are filled as soon as possible at the best available price. An investor cannot place a limit on the maximum price they will pay in the execution of this order, and because of that, this type of order would NOT be best utilized by an investor looking to limit or guard against a loss.

79. A: Futures commission merchants (FCMs) must handle all record keeping, including account confirmations and statements, for each of their accounts. The requirement for record keeping applies to the accounts of customers who are transacting business directly with an FCM as well as those accounts where the customer was introduced to the FCM by an introducing broker (IB). In the event an IB is involved, he or she is NOT required to maintain all of the appropriate records on customer accounts, although they may elect to do so. Both FCMs and IBs are required to maintain orders in a daily journal.

80. D: Futures contracts trading at an investor's limit price will NOT necessarily guarantee that the order was actually executed. There would always be the possibility that other orders for futures contracts were ahead at the same limit price. Limit orders can sometimes be referred to as "resting orders" at a time when the market is trading away from the specific contract's limit price. A sell limit order provides the investor the opportunity to set the minimum price he or she will accept in the sale of a futures contract, and it does not have guaranteed execution.

81. B: Communications are defined as including those distributed in hard copy or via electronic formats. Opinions may be given but must be clearly labeled as such. Hypothetical calculations cannot be utilized by members unless a specific enclosure regarding those calculations is included. Members must retain all of their written communications for five years, NOT three years, from the date when they last used them.

82. C: Buying back the position and closing it out at 65.75 will give us a 1.5 point gain on each contract from 67.25. Since this is a short position, we profit when the underlying decreases in market price. This 1.5 point gain is then multiplied by 100 since our contract size is 100 which gives us a $150 gain per contract. Multiply our $150 gain per contract by our total number of contracts of five to get $750 as the total gain on the position.

83. D: The correct way to enter a limit on open market order to buy 5 April wheat contracts with the price limit of 32.50 or better to be executed during the opening range of the market is "Buy 5 April wheat at 32.50 opening only."

84. A: The use of futures contracts provides both buyers and sellers with no immediate concern over large price swings due to locking in their prices to buy and sell in advance. Further, with their ability to operate more efficiently and reduce their business risk, sellers will see a reduction in commodity costs. These reduced costs will be passed along to buyers and ultimately the economy in the form of reduced prices for finished goods. With this reduction in business risk, all participating companies will be provided credit opportunities from lenders at lower, not higher rates.

85. B: An "exchange for physical order" involves the exchange of the physical underlying commodity for a futures contract. A "give up order" provides a customer the opportunity to remain anonymous in the transaction to protect their own identity, giving up the execution of the order to a futures commission merchant (FCM). A "bunched order" occurs with a single large order allocated out to the accounts of several different clients. There is no "market if exchanged order."

86. C: Delivery months for commodity futures contracts are set by exchanges on which the futures contract trades and are listed by both commodity and delivery month. Futures contracts cannot trade with delivery in all 12 calendar months and are listed with the nearest delivery month quoted first and more far-off months next from there.

87. A: A "limit or market on close" order to buy 7 September crude contracts at a price of 8.50 or better would be entered as "Buy 7 September crude at 8.50 or market on close." These types of orders provide for flexibility in the execution of the order in that the investor can initially designate the order be executed at a limit price or better and then, if not executed during the trading session, designate the order be changed to a market order for execution at the closing of the market. With this ability to change the type of order based on the pricing activity in the market, the investor is essentially guaranteeing the execution of the order during that trading session.

88. B: The minimum amount of margin required for continuing to hold a position is called the minimum maintenance margin. It is established by the exchange.

89. D: A "market if touched" order is also known as a "board order." The investor's intent by entering this order is to have the order executed if the market trades at or through their trigger price. It then becomes a market order to buy or sell at the next available price. An order to sell would strategically be entered above the market so as to possibly offset a long position.

90. B: Forward contracts are privately negotiated contracts to buy and sell either a commodity or financial instrument. Both the buyer and the seller are always obligated to perform according to the contractual obligations. The buyer has the obligation to accept delivery and pay at the contracted time and place, and the seller has the obligation to deliver the commodity in the agreed-upon amount at the contracted time and place. In the event that one of the original two parties fails to perform his or her contractual obligation, it is acceptable for another individual to take over the obligation, although difficult to do given that the contract had been specifically negotiated to meet the needs of the original two parties.

91. B: A scale order involves an investor either buying or selling futures contracts at specific intervals. It provides the investor the opportunity to buy and sell at an average price instead of one single price. A basis order is activated contingent upon some market event. A give up order has the investor remaining anonymous for the transaction, and a bunched order is an order executed on behalf of a group of clients.

92. D: S&P 500 futures are often used as a proxy to guess the opening direction of the U.S. stock market each day. Since futures trade 24/7, investors can look to see what the market looks like before it technically opens. If futures are up, chances are the market itself will open higher (but not always).

93. C: Individuals are required to own a membership to trade. Firms are NOT exempt from requirements held for individuals to trade on an exchange floor and in fact must have an association with someone who owns a membership to be considered as a member firm. Trading practices are regulated by the exchange itself, and buyers and sellers do NOT establish the margin requirements for their contracts. The exchanges themselves establish margin requirements on the contracts.

94. A: Counterparty risk is inherent in the transaction in that the seller bears the risk that the buyer won't pay or take delivery, and the buyer bears the risk that the seller will fail to deliver on the contract. Further, no entity exists to enforce the contract or compensate for the default of the obligation. Also, banks utilize forward contracts when doing business internationally. Forward contracts however cannot be obtained in a secondary market.

95. C: A properly entered "cancels former order" (CFO) would be "CFO Buy 9 April wheat at 8.25."

96. B: The futures exchange provides both producers and users the opportunity to hedge their risk, lock in prices for commodities, and manage aspects of their business. It does NOT provide producers and users the opportunity to negotiate contract specifics in that futures contracts have terms and conditions that are standardized by the exchange itself, and accordingly, determining the specifics of those contracts is out of the hands of the contracted parties.

97. A: "Market on open" orders allow for limit orders and, if not executed at the opening of the market, will be cancelled. Partial executions are allowed, and the "opening of the market" is NOT considered only the immediate time at the opening of the market but, instead, is a range of time defined by the exchange that qualifies as the opening of the trading day.

98. D: The terms and conditions of futures contracts are standardized and established by the exchanges, NOT negotiated specifically between the parties of the contract. Futures contracts, because of their standardized terms, can be traded in a secondary market. Futures contracts begin as a contract between two parties and can include the trading of financial instruments such as Treasury securities.

99. B: An investor buys 9 May corn contracts at a price of 2.25. They would like to sell their corn contracts higher to realize a profit but also seek a strategy that will protect them from suffering a loss on this position. The type of order that would best provide the strategy he or she is seeking is the "one order cancels the other" (OCO) order. Here he or she would enter the order "Sell 9 May corn at 2.85 or Sell 9 May corn at 2.25 stop." If the price of the corn contract rises to 2.85, the result would be the investor executing the order to sell 9 May corn contracts at 2.85, and then the order to sell at 2.25 would be cancelled.

100. A: A bunched order involves one single order executed for the accounts of several different clients. The allocation of the futures contracts can occur after the order's execution but must occur by the end of the trading day, NOT within 24 hours of the order's execution.

101. B: A commodity producer who has the commodity immediately on hand would be considered "long" the commodity. An individual who is under contract to deliver some amount of wheat but does not currently own wheat in that amount would be considered "short" the wheat commodity. A producer who has 290 barrels of oil would be considered "long" the 200 barrels of oil they do possess. A cattle farmer who needs corn to feed his cattle and who does not grow the corn him- or herself would be considered "short" the corn commodity in that he or she needs the corn to feed his cattle and has to continually obtain this commodity to conduct business.

102. D: In entering a "cancels former order" (CFO) order, this investor can change his or her original existing order in terms of its number of contracts or limit price or change the day order to a "good till cancel" (GTC) order.

103. C: Futures contracts have standardized terms and conditions, whereas forward contracts are privately negotiated. Because of standardized contracts, futures can be traded in a very liquid secondary market. Forwards have no secondary market. Futures contracts have no counterparty risk due to performance guarantees that compensate parties of the contract in the event that one party defaults or does not meet the obligation. Forward contracts have counterparty risk that is shared by both parties of the contract.

104. D: Floor traders may participate in day trading or take on long-term positions, and in the absence of any buy or sell orders to execute, they can opt not to execute any orders at all.

105. A: The commodity delivery process is determined by the exchange within which the commodity contract trades. Delivery cannot be made directly to the buyer even if all parties agree, and if multiple approved delivery locations are available, the buyer will NOT decide to which location they will accept delivery. In that case the seller of the commodity would choose which location delivery would be made to. Once delivery has been made, the commodity will be inspected for quality grade and quantity without any specific request made or intervention by the buyer.

106. C: A commodity futures option is a contract between two parties whereby the buyer pays a premium for the right to buy or sell a contract. Under this contract, the seller is NOT provided the "option" to perform under the contract, but instead he or she is obligated to perform under the contract.

107. B: Cornering the market is defined as the control, by an individual or group, of all or most of a commodity. If this were to occur, this individual or group would be in a position to name any price for that commodity and most likely get it. Marking to the market involves looking at the amount of margin on deposit versus the price on the futures contract and determining whether the position, now established, is still above the minimum maintenance level for the contract.

108. A: An investor of futures contracts will be said to have a "bearish" outlook if he or she believes that a specific futures contract price will be decreasing. With that belief, he or she will want to buy puts and sell calls to profit from locking in a higher sell price prior to the price decline. Buying calls and selling puts would be indicative of a "bullish" outlook (believing that the contract price will be increasing).

109. C: A buyer determining whether to establish a position in commodity futures should consider his or her maximum gain and loss for the transaction and what the breakeven on the transaction would be. The amount of premium that will be paid for the transaction is NOT a consideration given that the seller is paid the premium in the transaction, NOT the buyer.

110. D: An investor who purchases a futures contract put believes the futures contract price will decrease. If it does, the gain will come from buying at that lower price and exercising the option to sell at the higher option strike price. The potential maximum gain from this position is limited however in that the contract price is limited as to how far it can fall. The maximum gain will equal the contract strike price minus the premium.

111. C: The maximum gain on this position is simply the premium the investor was paid when he or she sold the call.

$$4 \times \$100 = \$400$$

The maximum loss on this position is unlimited. The investor in selling this call is hoping that the price of the underlying futures contract will decrease. In the event that it increases, the buyer of the call will want to exercise his or her option at the contracted lower price. Having sold this call short and without ownership of the underlying futures contract, the investor will then have to purchase the contract at the now-increased price to cover the call. Because the potential price increase of the contract is without limits, so too this investor's potential loss is also without limits.

$$Breakeven = Strike\ Price + Premium$$

$$\$704 = 700 + 4$$

112. D:

$$(\$.10 + \$.02) = \$.12\ total\ carrying\ cost\ for\ corn\ per\ bushel\ per\ month$$

$$(\$.12 \times 4) = \$.48\ total\ carrying\ cost\ for\ corn\ per\ bushel\ over\ 4\ months$$

$$(\$6.16 + \$.48) = \$6.64\ total\ cost\ per\ bushel\ to\ buy\ the\ corn\ and\ hold\ onto\ it\ for\ 4\ months$$

113. A: The investor's maximum gain on this position is unlimited in that profit on this position comes from an increase in the futures contract price. There is no limit on how high the price may increase, and accordingly, the potential gain has no limit also.

$$Breakeven = Strike\ Price + Premium$$

$$\$77 = 75 + 2$$

114. C: Members will report all transactions to the clearinghouse, and member firms will deposit the required margin, as calculated by the clearinghouse, by the next trading day's open. Futures contract trades settle the next business day, NOT the same business day.

115. B: An option seller is known as the "writer" and is "obligated" to perform under the contract, unlike the buyer, who always retains the "option" to exercise his or her rights (or not) under the contract. The seller's goal is to have the option expire without being exercised, thus providing him or her with what the main objective is, which is simply premium income. If the option is exercised the seller always runs the risk of loss of income in satisfying the obligation to sell or buy under the contract.

116. A: Investors might choose to purchase call options on futures contracts for different reasons. They may do it to simply profit from price appreciation on the futures contract, or if lacking the funds to purchase the contracts immediately, investors would seek to lock in a purchase price for futures contracts with the commodity to be delivered at a future date when they will possess the funds. Additionally, a user could utilize call options as a hedge against a price increase, NOT decrease for a commodity they know they will need in the future.

117. D: Options are classified as to their class (same type or same futures contract), type (call or put), and series (same class, same exercise price, or same expiration month).

118. A: All trading of futures contracts occurs in the pits; trades are then reported to the tape so as to be communicated to the marketplace, and if trading disputes occur, they would be resolved by the exchange's floor committee. Futures contracts may NOT be traded in the over-the-counter (OTC) market.

119. B: When considering a futures call option position's maximum gain or loss, the investor will profit from a rise in the price of the futures contract. His or her maximum gain would be unlimited, similar to if a futures contract had been purchased. The maximum loss would be limited to the premium paid for the option.

120. A: A call buyer's maximum loss is NOT unlimited. It is simply the premium paid to the seller of the call. If the price of the underlying contract decreases, the buyer will choose not to exercise the option to buy at what is the now higher option price. The option will then expire with the only loss being the cost of the premium paid to obtain that option. The call seller's maximum loss is unlimited, the buyer and the seller will break even at the same point, and a buyer's maximum gain is the seller's maximum loss. For both, that is "unlimited."

Practice Test #2

1. If an investor expects the price of a commodity to fall, all of the following would be appropriate actions EXCEPT:

a. The investor sells calls.
b. The investor buys puts.
c. Long the commodity.
d. Short the commodity.

2. Upon receipt of the notice of intent to deliver from a seller, the clearinghouse will have to determine which customer will be assigned the delivery notice to take delivery of the contract commodity. Which of the following is TRUE of how that may be done?

I. Assigned to the buyer with the most recently established open long position (last in, first out)
II. Assigned to the buyer with oldest open long position
III. Assigned to the buyer with the largest net long position
IV. Assigned to the buyer who can take delivery the soonest

a. I, II, III, and IV
b. II and III
c. II only
d. I and IV

3. Which of the following is defined as a purchased right to buy a futures contract at a specific price for a specified period of time?

a. Call option
b. Straddle
c. Put option
d. None of the above

4. Which of the following is TRUE regarding margin calculations?

a. Pricing changes on futures contracts have an effect on the amount of margin deposit required.
b. The clearinghouse is responsible for marking to the market.
c. Additional margin may be required if the deposit falls below the minimum maintenance amount on the contract.
d. All of the above are true.

5. Given normal market conditions, and the following table representing the wheat market at a specific point in time, which of the following would be the wheat contract price in October?

Cash Wheat	260
January	265
April	271
October	____
December	281

a. 278
b. 262
c. 269
d. 257

6. An investor purchased a call option on a futures contract. Which of the following is NOT a possible outcome for this transaction?

a. The call option is exercised.
b. The call option is sold.
c. The option contract is cancelled.
d. The option contract expires.

7. Which of the following would be in the same option class as a "Gold May 35 Call"?

I. Gold May 50 Call
II. Gold May 35 Put
III. Silver May 35 Call
IV. Gold August 36 Call

a. I, II, and IV
b. I and IV
c. II and III
d. I only

8. Which of the following is FALSE of the buyer of an option?

a. He or she is also known as the "owner."
b. The goal is to have the option exercised.
c. The purchase provides him or her the right to buy or sell.
d. The participation is for income purposes.

9. Which of the following statements is FALSE of the standard of "basis grade"?

a. If the seller delivers a commodity that is above this standard, he or she may require a premium paid upon delivery.
b. It is the minimum standard of quality set for a commodity to be considered good delivery under a futures contract.
c. The exchange will not allow a seller to deliver a commodity of a grade that is below this standard.
d. All of the above are true.

10. A user of wheat has the opportunity to either purchase wheat and store it until the time it's needed (three months from then) or purchase wheat futures with delivery to be accepted three months in the future. Which of the following is NOT a consideration as he or she chooses the option that will cost the least?

a. Total carrying cost for storing wheat over that time frame
b. Transportation cost for delivery
c. Price of wheat futures with delivery three months out
d. Price of wheat in the cash market

11. Which of the following is TRUE of a clearinghouse?

I. It facilitates clearing all commodity futures transactions.
II. It provides a limited guarantee of contract performance.
III. It virtually eliminates counterparty risk.
IV. It calculates margin requirement.

a. III only
b. I, III, and IV
c. I, II, III, and IV
d. II and IV

12. Which of the following would be in the same series of options as a "Silver March 40 Call"?

a. Silver May 35 Call
b. Silver March 35 Call
c. Silver March 45 Call
d. None of the above

13. Which of the following is FALSE regarding commodity delivery?

a. A notice of intent to deliver will contain the date for delivery, quantity, the grade to be delivered, and the location where delivery will be made.
b. The delivery can be only during the contracted month.
c. The first notice day is the first day in the contract month when delivery can be made.
d. All of the above are true.

14. Which of the following is defined as a member organization employee who executes orders both for him- or herself and for customer accounts?

a. Floor trader
b. Locals
c. Floor broker
d. Scalpers

15. A contango futures contract pricing structure would also be known as which of the following?

I. A premium market
II. A carrying charge market
III. An upward market
IV. A normal market

a. II only
b. II and IV
c. I, II, and IV
d. I and III

16. Which of the following does NOT accurately describe the futures market pricing structure?

a. The pricing trades above the price of the commodity itself.
b. The contract pricing is reduced the further out the delivery date goes.
c. The pricing for both the commodity and futures contracts tend to move in the same direction.
d. It is upward sloping.

17. Given a concern over wheat prices falling, a farmer would like to protect his or her profit by locking in a price for wheat. He or she sells a wheat futures contract to a speculator who believes the price of wheat is going to rise. Which of the following is FALSE regarding this scenario?

a. The speculator, given a change in his or her belief that wheat prices will rise, is still bound by the contract and obligated to proceed by its terms.
b. The futures contract obligates the farmer to deliver wheat and the speculator to purchase it.
c. Any change in the original wheat futures contract will not directly impact the farmer and his or her obligations on the contract.
d. All of the above are true.

18. Which of the following is TRUE of selling a futures call?

I. Breakeven is the strike price plus the premium.
II. The investor is obligated to perform under the contract if the buyer chooses to exercise his or her option.
III. The maximum gain is unlimited if the call is sold uncovered.
IV. The investor believes the underlying contract price will be decreasing.

a. I and III
b. II and IV
c. II and III
d. I, II, and IV

19. Clearinghouse member Smith Commodities establishes new long and short positions in corn futures all within the same trading day. Given their long position of 150 contracts and their short position of 40 contracts, what will be the amount of contracts for which the clearinghouse will require them to deposit margin on their netted position?

a. 190 contracts
b. 110 contracts
c. 150 contracts
d. 40 contracts

20. When considering hedgers and speculators, which of the following would be TRUE of the strategies utilized by them within the futures marketplace?

I. The speculator, believing commodity prices will fall, sells a futures contract, establishing a short position in that commodity.
II. The producer of a commodity, being long that commodity, sells futures in that commodity.
III. The speculator, believing commodity prices will rise, buys a futures contract establishing a long position in that commodity.
IV. The user of a commodity, being short that commodity, buys futures in that commodity.

a. I, II, III, and IV
b. IV only
c. II and III
d. I and II

21. Which of the following describes what occurs when an exchange requires that the buyer accept delivery of a commodity once notice has been assigned?

a. Stop order
b. Notice of required delivery
c. Stopped delivery notice
d. None of the above

22. With regard to a clearinghouse marking to the market, which of the following is TRUE?

I. If no trades have taken place, the settlement price is determined by taking the midpoint in the spread between the bid and the ask price.
II. If a futures position moves in favor of a member, which then results in the margin on deposit to be in excess of the margin required on the contract, the clearinghouse will accumulate the excess amount and carry it forward into future transactions for the member.
III. The contract price is taken from the exchange's published settlement price as of close on that trading day.
IV. The clearinghouse is prohibited from issuing a call for additional margin during the trading day.

a. I and III
b. III only
c. II and IV
d. I and II

23. Which of the following is FALSE of a bear call spread?

a. The strategy is to ensure maximum gain is unlimited.
b. The investor sells the call with the lower strike price and simultaneously buys the call with the higher strike price.
c. The investor believes that the futures contract price will fall.
d. All of the above are true.

24. Hedgers are defined by all of the following EXCEPT that

a. usually they are the users and producers of commodities.
b. their main objective is to make profit on futures contracts.
c. they utilize strategy to lock in prices to prevent loss of profit.
d. they seek to reduce risk.

25. An option's premium is made up of time value and intrinsic value. With respect to this, which of the following is FALSE?

I. An option's time value is the amount the option that is "in the money."
II. The time value equals the option's premium value above the intrinsic value.
III. An "out of the money" option has no intrinsic value.
IV. The time value is the price that is paid for the "option" or opportunity to buy or sell at the contracted price.

a. I, III, and IV
b. II and III
c. II and IV
d. I only

26. Which of the following is TRUE of a speculator's strategy?

I. The strategy involves taking a long futures position at a time when he or she anticipates the commodity value to decrease.
II. Anticipating news that would cause a probable increase in the future supply of a commodity would cause the speculator to establish a short futures position.
III. He or she utilizes a futures contract position to profit from the potential change in its value.
IV. The strategy is not risk averse.

a. II, III, and IV
b. I, II, and III
c. II and IV
d. I only

27. Which of the following is TRUE regarding the characteristics of a spread?

a. It involves simultaneous purchase of two options.
b. It involves two options with different exercise prices and/or different expiration months
c. It involves two options of different classes.
d. All of the following could be true.

28. How is open trade equity (OTE) calculated?

a. Initial margin deposit minus unrealized loss on the open contract position
b. Initial margin deposit plus unrealized profit or loss on the open contract position
c. Initial margin deposit plus unrealized loss on the open contract position
d. Initial margin deposit plus or minus unrealized profit or loss on the open contract position

29. Which of the following could be an example of a short hedger?

I. Jewelry manufacturer
II. Candy factory
III. Corn tortilla company
IV. Cattle ranch owner

a. IV only
b. I, II, III, and IV
c. II and III
d. I and IV

30. Bear put spreads are characterized by which of the following?

I. They are also known as debit put spreads.
II. They investor's maximum gain is unlimited.
III. The investor is looking to profit from a decrease in a futures contract price.
IV. The investor will purchase the put with the lower strike price and sell the put with the higher strike price.

a. III only
b. I, II, and IV
c. I and III
d. II and IV

31. Which of the following is TRUE regarding volatility and its impact on margin requirements?

I. An increase in maintenance requirements will only apply to new positions.
II. Initial margin requirements are established in part based on value at risk (VAR).
III. Minimal maintenance margins are established in part based on historical volatility calculations.
IV. Initial and maintenance requirements can be increased as volatility increases.

a. II, III, and IV
b. I, II, and IV
c. II and III
d. I only

32. A crude oil contract produces a profit of 6.70 per barrel. A total of three contracts were purchased. What is the total profit made excluding commissions?

a. $2,010
b. $26,800
c. $6,700
d. $20,100

33. A hedge's effectiveness will be dependent on which of the following?

I. Futures delivery months lining up with the producer's timing for producing the commodity
II. Correlation between the commodity price change and the change in the futures contract price
III. Futures delivery months lining up with the user's timing for needing the commodity
IV. Futures contract units being either more or less than the amount needing to be hedged

a. II only
b. I and III
c. I, II, III, and IV
d. II and IV

34. Which of the following is FALSE regarding the topic of a "margin"?

I. It may involve a loan being made to the customer.
II. The amount is set by the futures commission merchant.
III. The amount may vary depending on whether it's a long or short contract position and on the number of contracts.
IV. Money is deposited to establish a futures position.

a. II and III
b. I and II
c. II, III, and IV
d. I and IV

35. Which of the following is FALSE of customer accounts?

a. An under margined account allows for no withdrawals.
b. A customer's total equity equals the account balance plus or minus open trade equity.
c. A customer's account balance equals total deposits plus withdrawals.
d. A customer could establish a new position in an under margined account as long as the futures commission merchant believes he or she will provide the required funds for the new position margin and the funds for the margin call.

36. A crude oil contract produces a profit of 6.70 per barrel. With a total of three contracts purchased, profit per contract was $6,700, and the total profit on all contracts, excluding commissions, was $20,100. If a futures commission merchant charged this customer a commission of $35 per contract, what would the total net profit be, including the commission charge?

a. $19,995
b. $6,700
c. $13,435
d. $6,665

37. What would be the total required deposit if a trader were to purchase 6 May crude oil contracts and the initial margin requirement for crude oil is $6.22 a barrel?

a. $622
b. $3,732
c. $6,220
d. $37,320

38. An investor is awaiting significant news regarding the gold supply. Which of the following is TRUE regarding this scenario and what he or she may do next?

I. The investor should purchase 1 gold call.
II. The investor wants to profit from any extreme move in the price of gold that may result.
III. The investor should purchase a straddle.
IV. The investor will be concerned with only his or her maximum loss in determining the next investment move.

a. II and III
b. I only
c. III only
d. II, III, and IV

39. A customer who received a call for additional margin to be deposited into his or her account can obtain the required equity to restore the account by doing all of the following EXCEPT

a. transfer funds from an additional account.
b. obtain a loan from his or her futures commission merchant.
c. liquidate futures contracts.
d. deposit additional funds he or she obtained from the bank.

40. An investor establishes the following bull call spread:

- Long 1 December silver 1500 call at 5
- Short 1 December silver 1700 call at 2

To what amount is this investor reducing the maximum loss to by establishing this position?

a. 5
b. 2
c. 3
d. 7

41. Which of the following is TRUE regarding a maintenance margin?

a. Falling below the margin requires a deposit by the customer to restore the account to the initial margin requirement.
b. The margin is the minimum equity a customer is required to maintain to hold a futures position open.
c. Negative price changes will cause the margin balance to fall.
d. All of the above are true.

42. Which of the following is defined as the process by which a futures commission merchant will monitor the account equity of a margin account for changes that may occur due to futures contract price changes?

a. Marking to the market
b. Corner
c. Limit up
d. Offset

43. An option's premium is a measure of its value. Which of the following contributes to determining that premium?

a. Volatility of the underlying futures contract
b. Interest rates
c. Supply and demand
d. All of the above

44. Which of the following is FALSE of bull call spreads?

a. An investor believes that the futures contract price will decrease.
b. The strategy is to offset a possible loss of the premium paid for the long call.
c. It is considered a debit spread also.
d. The investor purchases a call with a lower strike price and simultaneously sells the call with the higher strike price.

45. A bakery is anticipating that in a few months (September), it will have the need for a large amount of wheat. The company is concerned that prices on wheat may increase dramatically over the next several months due to a shortage in supply, and does not see any significant probability of a price decrease. Which of the following should the bakery do to minimize wheat price risk?

a. Wait to purchase the amount of wheat needed when the time comes.
b. Purchase wheat futures for September delivery.
c. Purchase the amount of wheat they anticipate needing in the spot market, take delivery of it, and store it for the next few months until needed.
d. Either B or C.

46. What type of spread is defined as one long option and one short option of the same class and with different expiration months and strike prices?

a. Calendar spread
b. Diagonal spread
c. Vertical spread
d. Price spread

47. Which of the following is FALSE of a speculator?

a. The strategy involves injecting risk capital into the futures market.
b. The goal is to profit from "speculations" regarding future commodity price movements.
c. They can be large funds as well as individual investors.
d. They seek to minimize or eliminate risk.

48. Established position:

- Buy 2 July crude oil at 78 and Sell 2 July crude oil at 75.5.
- Calculate the loss (excluding commissions) per barrel, the loss per contract, and the total loss of all contracts, on this position if crude oil were trading at 78 and, due to a slight increase in supply, dropped by 2.50.

a. $25, $25,000, $50,000
b. $2.50, $2,500, $5,000
c. $.25, $250, $500
d. None of the above

49. There are two types of hedgers, long and short. Long hedgers are all of the following EXCEPT that they

a. could be a user of the commodity.
b. would be "short the basis" if they are in a position to be obligated to deliver the physical commodity.
c. purchase futures to protect against the risk associated with a commodity price decrease.
d. could be someone who does not own the commodity but who is contractually obligated to deliver it.

50. Which of the following is FALSE regarding the role margin plays in establishing a futures position?

a. There are some futures contracts that do not require a margin account.
b. A customer having purchased a futures contract will observe his or her margin balance increase as the contract price increases.
c. To ensure that a customer's margin balance remains above its minimum maintenance level, the futures commission merchant will be observing the futures contract's price movement.
d. It varies from contract to contract in that it's based on a percentage of the total contract value.

51. Which of the following are FALSE of a hedger?

a. He or she utilizes profits made from futures contracts to offset the effects of adverse commodity price changes.
b. He or she seeks to profit from futures contract positions.
c. He or she utilizes futures to take the position that is opposite of whatever the position in the underlying commodity is.
d. Users or producers of a commodity seek to reduce business risk.

52. An investor has a 2 contract position that (excluding commissions) had a per-contract loss of $2,500 and a total loss of $5,000. What would the per-contract loss and total loss be, including a commission charge of $40?

a. $2,460, $4,920
b. $2,000, $4,000
c. $2,540, $5,080
d. $2,500, $5,000

53. Which of the following is FALSE regarding options on Treasury bill futures and their premiums?

a. Options are based on $100,000 par value of a 13-week Treasury bill
b. The premium must be divided by four to determine the final amount owed by the investor.
c. The premium is quoted as an annualized percentage of par value.
d. All of the above are true.

54. Which of the following is TRUE regarding the relationship between an option's strike price and the price of the underlying contract for calls and puts?

I. The "in the money" put, strike price is less than the futures contract price.
II. The "in the money' call, futures contract price is greater than strike price.
III. The "out of the money" put, futures contract price is greater than the strike price.
IV. The "at the money" put, futures contract price equals the strike price.

a. I and III
b. II only
c. II, III, and IV
d. I, III, and IV

55. Which of the following is FALSE of a short hedger?

a. He or she could be the producer of the commodity.
b. He or she sells futures to protect against the risk of an increase in the commodity price.
c. He or she may be someone who actually owns the commodity.
d. A commodity producer would be considered being "long the basis."

56. Which of the following is TRUE of the maximum loss on a long straddle?

a. Maximum loss occurs only when a futures contract price at expiration equals the strike price of both options.
b. Maximum loss is limited to the total premium paid.
c. The total premium equals the call premium plus put premium.
d. All of the above are true.

57. In consideration of straddles, which of the following is TRUE?

I. The long straddle maximum gain is the total premium.
II. The short straddle breakeven equals the strike price plus or minus total premium.
III. The long straddle breakeven equals the strike price plus or minus the total premium.
IV. The short straddle maximum loss is unlimited.

a. I and II
b. I only
c. II, III, and IV
d. III and IV

58. Which of the following is an example of a price spread?

a. Short 1 March wheat 75 call, Long 1 April wheat 60 call
b. Short 1 June gold 700 put, Long 1 August gold 850 put
c. Short 1 May silver 1100 call, Long 1 October silver 1100 call
d. Long 1 September corn 350 put, Short 1 September corn 250 put

59. A trader sells 5 November gold at 1785 AND buys 5 November gold at 1779. What is the profit per ounce, profit per contract, and total profit of all contracts (excluding commissions)?

a. $6, $60, $300
b. $30, $3,000, $15,000
c. $6, $600, $3,000
d. unknown, not enough information to determine

60. Which of the following is FALSE regarding the relationship between an option's strike price and the price of the underlying futures contract?

a. An in the money call option has a futures contract price that is greater than the option strike price.
b. It contributes to the overall profitability of the option position.
c. An at the money put option has a futures contract price that is equal to the option strike price.
d. An out of the money call option has a futures contract price that is lower than the option strike price.

61. Given the following long straddle, determine the breakeven point for the call and the put.

- Long 1 May corn 200 Call at .45
- Long 1 May corn 200 Put at .41

a. Call 286, Put 114
b. Call 208.60, Put 191.40
c. Call 286, Put 286
d. None of the above

62. Considering a long straddle, which of the following is FALSE?

a. An investor anticipates extreme volatility in the futures contract price.
b. An investor is not bullish or bearish when taking this position.
c. It is a simultaneous purchase of a call and put on the same futures contract.
d. The position involves different expiration months but the same strike price.

63. What would the maximum gain be on the following bull call spread?

- Long 1 May wheat 35 call at 6
- Short 1 May wheat 50 call at 2

a. 13
b. 11
c. 9
d. 15

64. An investor sells a put. Which of the following is FALSE if the underlying futures contract price falls?

a. The contract price falling to zero is the worst-case scenario for the investor.
b. It limits the maximum loss for the investor.
c. The investor will not receive the contract premium.
d. All of the above are true.

65. Which of the following must be considered when determining the profit or loss on a speculative futures position?

I. Number of contracts
II. Number of units per contract
III. Price at which contract was opened
IV. Price per unit per contract

a. I and II
b. I, II, III, and IV
c. I, II, and IV
d. III and IV

66. A "time spread" is another name for which spread?

a. Calendar spread
b. Price spread
c. Diagonal spread
d. Vertical spread

67. A September 45 call, trading at $41, and with a premium of $3—given this call is "out of the money," what would its intrinsic and time value be?

a. $2 intrinsic value, $1 time value
b. no intrinsic value, $3 time value
c. $4 intrinsic value, $3 time value
d. Unknown due to lack of information to determine

68. What would be the breakeven on the following bull call spread?

- Long 1 November corn 40 call at 10
- Short 1 November corn 60 call at 7

a. 37
b. 50
c. 47
d. 43

69. A report regarding wheat production is due out in the next few days. March wheat is trading at $3. There's an investor with no knowledge of whether the report will be positive or negative for wheat production. Which of the following positions should this investor establish so as to provide the highest chance of profitability?

a. Long 1 March wheat 300 Call at .75, Long 1 May wheat 300 Put at .70
b. Long 1 March wheat 300 Put at .25
c. Long 1 March wheat 300 Call at .25, Long 1 March wheat 300 Put at .22
d. None of the above

70. Price spreads are utilized in determining which of the following?

I. Whether the investor will want to exercise the option or let it expire
II. Maximum loss
III. Breakeven point
IV. Whether the position results in a net credit or debit

a. I and IV
b. II and III
c. IV only
d. I, II, III, and IV

71. A speculator establishes a Long 1 March corn contract at 45. Due to issues with a decreased crop supply, the March delivery price increases to 53. The resulting close-out position is a sale of 1 corn contract at 53. What would be the profit on this position?

a. 3
b. 5
c. 8
d. Unknown, due not enough information

72. Which of the following are TRUE of a put buyer verse a put seller?

I. A put buyer's maximum loss is the premium paid to the seller.
II. A put buyer's breakeven is the strike price minus the premium.
III. A put seller's maximum gain is the premium received from the buyer.
IV. A put seller's intent and hope are that the option is exercised.

a. IV only
b. I, II, and III
c. I and III
d. II and IV

73. What is the premium on a November Treasury bond futures 95 call that is being quoted at 1.16?

a. $12.50
b. $1,025
c. $1,250
d. $1,160

74. Which of the following points are FALSE of a short straddle?

I. The investor is more concerned with whether the price of the contract increases or decreases, not the significance of the move.
II. The investor will usually take this position after a period of low volatility, believing that level of volatility will continue.
III. The investor's investment outlook is either bearish or bullish.
IV. The investor believes the price of the futures contract will trade with minimal volatility, with no significant moves up or down.

a. II, III, and IV
b. I, II, and III
c. I and IV
d. I only

75. Which of the following would be considered an "in the money" option?

a. January gold 97 call, January gold is trading at 109
b. February wheat 70 call, February wheat is trading at 57
c. July silver 155 call, June silver is trading at 170
d. October corn 45 call, October corn is trading at 45

76. What is the premium on a Treasury bill futures option that is being quoted at 2.5 percent?

a. $2,500
b. $6,250
c. $250
d. $625

77. Which of the following is FALSE of the "basis"?

a. It is quoted as the relationship between the commodity price and the price of the futures contract.
b. The direction of spread change will either strengthen or weaken the basis.
c. It is the difference between the cash commodity price and the near-term futures contract.
d. It strengthens as it becomes less positive.

78. Which of the following is NOT accurate of S&P 500 futures contracts?

a. They are appropriate for hedging a large diverse portfolio.
b. They are the most efficient hedge against nonsystematic risk.
c. The profits from a short S&P position can help to offset loss due to a decline in portfolio value.
d. They could be utilized by portfolio and pension plan managers.

79. A commodity's crop year is the center point of its agricultural contracts. Which of the following statements is TRUE?

I. A commodity's harvest period involves the time when the crop is mature enough to then be prepped for delivery.
II. Not all producers of a given commodity are subject to the same commodity growing season.
III. A commodity's crop year starts at harvest time and ends with the commodity's harvest period of the next year.
IV. Regulations are put in place to spread out the release of the supply of a given commodity to the market over a long range of time rather than all at once.

a. I and III
b. I and II
c. III and IV
d. II and IV

80. Which of the following is the appropriate pricing unit for live cattle?

a. 40,000 pounds
b. 112,000 pounds
c. 50,000 pounds
d. 80,000 pounds

81. Which of the following is FALSE regarding open interest in a futures contract?

a. Higher liquidity means smaller spreads for the contract.
b. Changes in open interest will always confirm whatever trend is being observed in the market.
c. Decreased open interest indicates that market participants are exiting.
d. Higher open interest means higher liquidity in that contract.

82. In the event of a commodity supply shortage, which of the following is FALSE?

a. Demand for the commodity and for the near-term contracts increases.
b. Backwardation occurs.
c. It's a good opportunity for selling distant futures contracts for profit.
d. Market for commodity may become inverted.

83. Which of the following statements is TRUE of futures market pricing?

I. Pricing for futures trade below the commodity price.
II. Commodity and futures contracts (near-term and distant) pricing usually all move in the same direction.
III. There is an upward sloping relationship between physical commodity and the futures market.
IV. As delivery dates extend further into the future, pricing for futures contracts increase.

a. II, III, and IV
b. III and IV
c. I and II
d. I, III, and IV

84. Calculate the beta-adjusted value at risk of a portfolio if the portfolio's value is $75 million with a portfolio beta of 1.7.

a. $44,118,000
b. $127,500
c. $127,500,000
d. $1,275

85. Which of the following is TRUE regarding the pricing and sizing of futures contracts?

I. The contract "tick" is based solely on the contract's pricing.
II. The exchange sets the maximum amount by which the futures contract value can change within a session of trading.
III. The exchange sets a minimum price variation for a contract.
IV. The limit up-limit down rule is also known as the daily price limit.

a. I and IV
b. II and III
c. II, III, and IV
d. I only

86. Which of the following is TRUE of US Treasury futures?

a. Contracts are backed by the US government.
b. They are traded on the Chicago Board of Trade (CBOT).
c. They cover $100,000 par value of US Treasury bonds with maturities of at least 20 years from the delivery date.
d. All of the above are true.

87. Two types of risk that portfolio managers work to hedge against include systematic and nonsystematic risk. Which of the following are TRUE of systematic risk?

I. It is diversifiable.
II. An example would be rising inflation.
III. It is inherent to the entire market.
IV. It means market volatility.

a. II, III, and IV
b. I only
c. I, II, III, and IV
d. III only

88. Which of the following commodity contracts is NOT priced in units representing 5,000 bushels?

a. Wheat
b. Sugar
c. Soybean
d. Corn

89. Which of the following is FALSE of a commodity's crop year?

a. If current crop is still abundant and forecasts for next year are lower, the current harvest month's contract may be priced higher than the month before it.
b. Forecasted production for the next year relative to the current year impacts contract pricing.
c. During a normal market, the commodity contract price for the harvest month will be higher than the month before it.
d. Commodity prices are usually at their lowest during the harvest period.

90. Which of the following is TRUE of an exporter selling product overseas who will be receiving payment in foreign currency and the risks associated with that?

I. Currency value falling, worth fewer US dollars, reduces the effective sale price of good sold.
II. The hedge involves an exporter selling foreign currency futures.
III. He or she is concerned with the dollar rising relative to the foreign currency he or she is to receive as payment.
IV. The exporter would be considered a short hedger if selling currency futures.

a. I, III, and IV
b. I and II
c. IV only
d. I, II, III, and IV

91. Which of the following commodity contracts is NOT priced in "cents per pound"?

a. Coffee
b. Orange juice
c. Cocoa
d. Sugar

92. In a normal market, futures contracts pricing increases the further out delivery months go. Which of the following is FALSE regarding futures pricing?

a. As the delivery month draws closer, the commodity price and spot futures contract price will drift further apart.
b. Delivery months that are further out have higher pricing due to a carrying charge.
c. Pricing for delivery months are considered to be trading at a "premium" to the commodity.
d. During the actual delivery period, the contract price will be the same as the commodity price.

93. Which of the following is FALSE of S&P 500 stock index futures?

a. The contract value is $150 times the contract price.
b. Contracts trade in minimum increments of $0.10.
c. They provide investors with broad exposure to the bigger market by placing one order.
d. It is a highly liquid market.

94. Which of the following chart patterns prevents a price drop from declining further?

a. Resistance
b. Support
c. Reversals
d. None of the above

95. The Commodity Futures Trading Commission (CFTC) and the Chicago Board of Trade (CBOT) provide reports of the grain supply. Which of the following is FALSE regarding this supply report?

a. Grain is counted as visible supply as it moves off the farm.
b. Any change to the visible supply report is an indication of a potential surplus or shortage.
c. If a supply is seen increasing, it could be an indication of an impending price decline.
d. It is published daily to help forecast futures prices.

96. The visible supply grain report does NOT include which of the following?

a. Grains that are in transit
b. Grain that remains on the farm
c. Grains in storage elevators
d. Grains on loading docks

97. Which of the following pricing characteristics are chosen with the production of the specific commodity in mind?

a. Pricing increments
b. The amount of underlying commodity to be covered
c. The expiration months that will be traded
d. All of the above

98. Which of the following is a reason for an investor to sell foreign currency futures?

a. A large quantity of a valuable commodity is discovered within that foreign country.
b. There is a dramatic rise in that foreign country's stock market.
c. Unemployment in that foreign country goes down.
d. A political event occurs that results in an increase in political instability in that foreign country.

99. Which of the following commodity contracts does NOT have delivery months that are structured as consecutive months for some varying, extended length of time?

a. Natural gas
b. Copper
c. Corn
d. Crude

100. Commodity users are characteristically which of the following?

I. They would like the basis to widen.
II. They are short hedgers.
III. They need to acquire the commodity.
IV. They would like futures prices to go up.

a. I and III
b. II only
c. I, III, and IV
d. II and IV

101. Which of the following is FALSE of technical analysis?

a. Charts are a significant tool in their analysis.
b. Commodity usage will not be considered.
c. An analyst can utilize patterns seen in past commodity price performance to forecast pricing direction going forward.
d. An analyst will examine the fundamentals of the commodity's market.

102. A commodity's carrying charge is made up of which of the following?

I. Interest expenses on borrowed funds
II. Insurance
III. Exchange fees
IV. Storage fees

a. III and IV
b. I, II, and IV
c. IV only
d. I, II, and III

103. The owner of a wheat farm made a best-guess prediction for his next crop at 126,000 bushels. If trying to hedge utilizing futures contracts that cover 8,000 bushels of wheat, how many contracts should he sell to hedge his entire crop?

a. 15.75
b. 15
c. 16
d. None of the above

104. When managing portfolios with holdings included in a variety of indexes, futures in those indexes can be utilized to hedge risk. Which of the following indexes could be utilized to hedge such a portfolio?

a. NASDAQ 100
b. Russell 2,000
c. Nikkei 225
d. All of the above

105. In a market where open interest is going up, which of the following is FALSE?

a. If commodity price is falling, new market participants are dominated by sellers driving prices lower.
b. If the price of a commodity is increasing, new market participants are dominated by buyers driving prices higher.
c. If the price of a commodity is increasing, it is a weak market overall.
d. All of the above are true.

106. A hedge's profit or loss has an effect on a commodity's selling price. Considering that, which of the following is FALSE?

a. Any gains from a commodity user's hedge will reduce the commodity's effective cost.
b. Knowing when to remove a hedge is not important to its effectiveness.
c. Timing for when to establish a hedge is critical to its effectiveness.
d. Profit from a commodity producer's hedge will increase the commodity's effective selling price.

107. Currency hedges are utilized by those who do business internationally. Which of the following is FALSE of a currency hedge?

a. A business needing to make payment in a foreign currency will fear the value of the dollar going up.
b. A strong dollar is good for buying goods from overseas.
c. Currency value changes can impact profits and costs.
d. A company purchasing products overseas might purchase foreign currency futures as a long hedge.

108. Which of the following is TRUE of a reversal pattern?

I. A bearish reversal shows an end of a downward trend and start of a new upward trend.
II. Head and shoulders top is bearish.
III. It indicates a significant commodity price change in trend.
IV. Head and shoulders bottom reverses a down trend.

a. II and IV
b. I and III
c. II, III, and IV
d. I only

109. Which of the following chart patterns indicates buyers and sellers looking to trade a commodity at virtually the same price?

a. Support
b. Resistance
c. Reversal
d. None of the above

110. Which of the following is FALSE regarding an interest rate hedge?

a. A hedger could buy Treasury bond futures and establish a long hedge.
b. Interest rates drop, and the price of outstanding bonds drops.
c. A hedger would be seeking to protect against an interest rate drop and what that might mean to the investment he or she is intending to make at a future time.
d. If the price of the bonds goes up, the investor would have to pay more for the bond and have a lower current yield and lower yield to maturity.

111. Which of the following is TRUE of open interest?

a. It is an indicator of a market's strength.
b. It aids in signaling the futures market direction.
c. It is the total of outstanding contracts that have yet to be closed or offset.
d. All of the above are true.

112. All of the following describe nonsystematic risk EXCEPT:

a. The strategy might involve having a hedge fund that is short equities, hedging against a market increase by purchasing S&P 500 futures.
b. Can be hedged against by diversifying amongst issuers or securities.
c. It is the risk inherent in the market.
d. It can be diversified away.

113. Which of the following is TRUE regarding the potential strength or weakness of the basis?

a. As the spread moves more negatively, the stronger the basis actually becomes.
b. When the commodity price is less than the price of the futures contract, the commodity has a positive basis.
c. When the commodity price is greater than price of the futures contract, the commodity has a negative basis.
d. None of the above is true.

114. "Front month" would be described as which of the following?

I. The first month in the calendar year for delivery in a given commodity
II. The futures contract with the earliest delivery date
III. The contract that is quoted the most
IV. The contract with the highest amount of trading volume

a. I only
b. II, III, and IV
c. II only
d. III and IV

115. Which of the following is FALSE of commodity producers?

a. They are long hedgers.
b. They are "long" the commodity.
c. They would like the basis to become less negative.
d. They would like the commodity price to increase.

116. Portfolio managers may hedge based on their portfolio's beta. Which of the following is TRUE of a beta hedge?

a. A beta less than one is considered to be more risky.
b. Beta-adjusted value is found by taking the value of the portfolio and multiplying it by the portfolio's beta.
c. A beta greater than one has a volatility level that is lower than the market.
d. A portfolio's beta is its projected rate of change as it is relative to a specific segment of the market.

117. Which of the following is FALSE of interest rate hedgers?

a. Short hedging here could involve selling Treasury bond futures.
b. Motivation may come from a need to borrow money at a future date through bond issuance.
c. They hedge against the risk of interest rates going down.
d. All of the above are true.

118. Of the following, which involve risks that can be hedged by futures contracts?

a. Interest rate risk
b. Currency risk
c. Stock market price decline
d. All of the above

119. "Basis grade" is which of the following?

I. Premium
II. Standard
III. Maximum
IV. Minimum

a. I and III
b. II and IV
c. I only
d. III only

120. In a market where open interest is going down, which of the following is FALSE?

a. If the price of a commodity is also decreasing, it is a weak market overall.
b. If the price of a commodity is also increasing, short positions are being covered faster than the start of new positions.
c. If a commodity price is falling, the result would be a liquidating market.
d. All of the above are true.

Answer Key and Explanations

1. C: If an investor expects the price of a commodity to fall, then appropriate actions to take in order to profit would be to sell calls, buy puts, or short the contract. All of these positions benefit when the underlying decreases in value. Going long the commodity or security would lose money in the event that it declines in value so this position would not make sense.

2. B: Upon receipt of the notice of intent to deliver from a seller, the clearinghouse will have to determine which customer will be assigned the delivery notice to take delivery of the contract commodity. Depending on the exchange, the delivery notice may be assigned to either the buyer with oldest open long position or the buyer with the largest net long position.

3. A: A call option is a purchased right to buy a futures contract at a specific price for a specified period of time. A put option is a purchased right to sell a futures contract at a specific price for a specified period of time. A straddle involves buying or selling a call and a put at the same time, on the same security, with both with the same strike price and expiration.

4. D: The clearinghouse is responsible for marking to the market. This involves looking at the amount of margin on deposit versus the price on the futures contract. The question is whether the position, now established, is still above the minimum maintenance level for the contract. Pricing changes on futures contracts have an effect on the amount of margin deposit that will be required. Additional margin may be required if the deposit falls below the minimum maintenance amount.

5. A: Given normal market conditions, and the information provided in the table, the wheat contract price in October would be 278. Normal market conditions dictate that contract prices be trading above the price of the cash commodity. Further, all successive prices must increase the farther out in delivery month you go. Here the price of cash wheat is 260. The 278 price is the only choice that is both higher than the cash wheat price of 260, and above the April price of 271, but below the December price of 281.

6. C: An investor purchases a call option on a futures contract. There are three possible outcomes for this transaction. First, the call option can be exercised by the investor, which involves exercising the contractual right to buy futures under the contract. Second, the investor may decide to sell the rights under the contract to another investor, and third, the investor may decide to NOT exercise the rights under the contract and let it simply expire. These are the only outcomes for this investor, given that the option contract cannot be expressly cancelled.

7. B: Options within the same option class must be of the same type (call or put) and be for the same underlying futures contract. Here the options that would be in the same option class as "Gold May 35 Call" are Gold May 50 Call and Gold August 36 Call.

8. D: The buyer of an option is also known as the "owner." The purchase provides him or her the right to buy or sell, depending on whether it is a call or put. The goal is to have the option exercised, NOT expire unexercised. Participation is speculative in nature in that the buyer has a belief in the direction a contract's price will go and would like to profit from that through the purchase of either a call or put. Exercising the option means that the contract price moved in the direction he or she believed it would. The buyer is NOT purchasing an option for income purposes.

9. C: A basis grade is the minimum standard of quality set for a commodity to be considered good delivery under a futures contract. The exchange will allow a seller to deliver a commodity of a grade that is below this standard, but it will be for a discounted price. If the seller delivers a commodity that is above this standard, the seller may require a premium paid for it upon delivery.

10. B: A user of wheat has the opportunity either to purchase wheat and store it until the time it's needed (three months from then), or to purchase wheat futures with delivery to be accepted three months in the future. Factors that he or she should consider in ensuring that he or she chooses the option that will cost the least are, first, the price of wheat in the cash market plus the total carrying cost for storing that wheat over the three-month time frame and, second, the price of wheat futures with delivery being accepted three months out. Looking at these factors will allow him or her to compare the total cost of purchase and storage of the wheat for three months versus the cost of purchasing the wheat and taking delivery three months later. The transportation cost for delivery of the wheat is not a factor in determining which of these options will cost the least, since the cost is assumed to be the same in these types of calculations for exam purposes unless stated otherwise.

11. B: Commodity exchanges utilize clearinghouses to facilitate clearing all of their commodity futures transactions. In providing a full, NOT limited, guarantee of contract performance, the clearinghouse virtually eliminates counterparty risk for both the buyer and the seller of a contract barring extreme circumstances. Clearinghouses are also responsible for calculating the margin requirements member firms must deposit upon contract settlement.

12. D: An option series would only include options that are of the same class (same type and same underlying futures contract), same exercise price, and same expiration month. Here all three are of the same class but have different exercise prices and/or expiration months.

13. D: Delivery can be made only during the stated month on the contract; the "first notice day" is the first day in the contract month when delivery can be made, and a notice of intent to deliver will contain the date for delivery, quantity and grade to be delivered, and the location where delivery will be made.

14. C: A floor broker is defined as a member organization employee who executes orders for both themselves and for customer accounts. A floor trader is an exchange member who executes trades for his or her own account. The terms "locals" and "scalpers" are also used to refer to a floor trader.

15. C: A contango futures contract pricing structure would also be known as a premium market, a carrying charge market, and a normal market. This type of pricing structure is one in which futures contracts trade at higher prices the further out their delivery month is.

16. B: The futures market pricing structure is upward sloping with pricing trading above the price of the commodity itself. The contract pricing is increased, NOT reduced, the further out the delivery date goes. Pricing for both the commodity and futures contracts tend to move in the same direction.

17. D: This futures contract obligates the farmer to deliver wheat and the speculator to purchase it. The speculator, given a change in his belief that wheat prices will rise is still bound by the contract and obligated to proceed by the terms of the contract. The speculator has the option to sell the wheat contract, relieving himself of the obligation on the contract. Any change in the original wheat futures contract will not directly impact the farmer and his obligations on the contract in that the wheat he contracted to deliver will still be matched by the clearinghouse with another speculator looking to take delivery within same time frame.

18. D: An investor selling a futures call believes the underlying contract price will be decreasing. If it does, the option will not be exercised, and the investor's gain is the premium paid when selling the option. If the buyer chooses to exercise the option, the investor will be obligated to perform under the contract. The investor's breakeven on this position will be the strike price plus the premium if at expiration the contract price increases by the same amount as the option premium paid. The maximum gain if the call is sold uncovered is NOT unlimited. The gain received would result from the option not being exercised, and accordingly it would be limited to only the premium paid when the investor sold the call.

19. B: Clearinghouse member Smith Commodities establishes new long and short positions in corn futures all within the same trading day. Given the long position of 150 contracts and the short position of 40 contracts, the clearinghouse will require Smith to deposit margin on 110 contracts. The clearinghouse will be calculating the amount of margin required for deposit based on Smith's netted position.

$$150 \textit{ long contracts} - 40 \textit{ short contracts} = 110 \textit{ contracts}$$

20. A: A speculator believing commodity prices will fall sells a futures contract establishing a short position in that commodity. If the price falls, he or she will benefit from purchasing low and delivering at the higher contract price. A producer of a commodity, being long that commodity, sells futures to lock in the price and protect the profit from a potential fall in prices for that commodity. A speculator believing commodity prices will rise buys a futures contract establishing a long position in that commodity with plans to profit from the appreciation of that contract. A user of a commodity, being short that commodity, buys futures in that commodity to lock in the current price and guard against any possible rise in prices later.

21. C: When an exchange requires that a buyer accept delivery of a commodity once notice has been assigned to it, it is known as a stopped delivery notice. With this notice the buyer would further be prohibited from offsetting the delivery requirement by selling a futures contract in the same delivery month to another buyer.

22. A: With regard to a clearinghouse marking to the market, the contract price utilized is taken from the exchange's published settlement price as of close on that trading day. If no trades have taken place, the settlement price is determined by taking the midpoint in the spread between the bid and the ask price. If a futures position moves in favor of a member, which then results in the margin on deposit to be in excess of the margin required on the contract, the clearinghouse will NOT accumulate the excess amount and carry it forward into future transactions for the member. They instead will simply return the excess to the member. In the event there is the need for additional margin, the clearinghouse can issue a call for it during that trading day.

23. A: A bear call spread involves an investor selling a call with a lower strike price and simultaneously buying a call with a higher strike price. The investor believes that the futures contract price will fall, and their strategy for establishing the position is to ensure that the maximum loss is limited.

24. B: Hedgers seek to reduce risk. They usually are the users and producers of commodities whose main objective is NOT to make profit on futures contracts but instead utilize futures contracts as a strategy to lock in prices to prevent loss of profit.

25. D: An option's premium is made up of time value and intrinsic value. An option's intrinsic value, NOT its time value, is the amount the option is "in the money." The time value equals the option's premium value above the intrinsic value and is the price that is paid for the "option" or opportunity to buy or sell at the contracted price. An "out of the money" option has no intrinsic value.

26. A: A speculator utilizes a futures contract position to profit from the potential change in its value. He or she is NOT risk averse in that he or she seeks to take on risk while seeking profit. In anticipating news that would cause a probable increase in the future supply of a commodity would cause the speculator to establish a short futures position. This is because of the probable price decline that would result from the commodity supply increase. The strategy involves taking a long futures position at a time when he or she anticipates the commodity value to increase, NOT decrease.

27. D: Spreads are the purchase or sale of two or more options. There are debit and credit spreads, horizontal and vertical spreads, etc.

28. D: Open trade equity (OTE) is calculated by taking the initial margin deposit and then adding or subtracting the unrealized profit or loss on the open contract position.

29. A: A short hedger either produces the commodity or owns it. With that, the cattle ranch owner would be considered a short hedger. By way of operating a cattle ranch, he or she owns the cattle commodity. The jewelry manufacturer, candy factory, and corn tortilla company would all be considered long hedgers in that they are all users of a commodity (gold, sugar, and corn) but do not own it themselves.

30. C: A bear put spread is established by an investor looking to profit from a decrease in a futures contract price. He or she will purchase the put with the higher strike price and sell the put with the lower strike price. The investor, by establishing this position, will be limiting the maximum gain in that the profit from any decline past the lower put's strike price will be received by the investor who that put was sold to, NOT the investor who established the spread.

31. A: Initial margin requirements are established in part based on value at risk (VAR), and minimal maintenance margins are established in part based on historical volatility calculations. Initial and maintenance requirements can be increased as volatility increases, but any increase that occurs will apply to new positions as well as any open contract positions.

32. D: Each oil contract represents 1,000 barrels of oil.

$$Profit\ per\ contract = profit\ per\ barrel \times 1{,}000\ barrels$$

$$Profit\ per\ contract = 6.70 \times 1{,}000 = \$6{,}700$$

$$Total\ profit\ on\ all\ contracts = profit\ per\ contract \times \#\ of\ contracts$$

$$Total\ profit\ on\ all\ contracts = \$6{,}700 \times 3 = \$20{,}100$$

33. C: A hedge's effectiveness will in part be dependent on the futures delivery months lining up with the producer's timing for producing the commodity or the futures delivery months lining up with the user's timing for needing the commodity. The correlation between the commodity price change and the change in the futures contract price will be impactful, as will be whether the futures contract units are either more or less than the amount needing to be hedged.

34. B: Margin is the money to be deposited to establish a futures position. It is an amount set by the exchange's board of directors, NOT the futures commission merchant. There is no loan ever made to the customer.

35. C: A customer's account balance equals total deposits minus withdrawals. A customer's total equity equals the account balance plus or minus open trade equity. An under margined account allows for no withdrawals. A customer could establish a new position in an under margined account as long as the futures commission merchant believes he or she will provide the required funds for the new position margin and the funds for the margin call.

36. A:

$$Total\ net\ profit\ per\ contract\ = total\ profit\ per\ contract - commission\ per\ contract$$

$$Total\ net\ profit\ per\ contract\ = \$6{,}700 - \$35\ = \$6{,}665$$

$$Total\ net\ profit\ on\ all\ contracts\ = total\ profit\ per\ contract\ \times \#\ of\ contracts$$

$$Total\ net\ profit\ on\ all\ contracts\ = \$6{,}665\ \times 3\ = \$19{,}995$$

37. D: Each crude oil contract represents 1,000 barrels of oil.

$$Initial\ margin\ requirement\ per\ contract\ = initial\ margin\ requirement\ \times 1{,}000\ barrels$$

$$Initial\ margin\ requirement\ per\ contract\ = 6.22\ \times 1{,}000\ = \$6{,}220$$

$$Total\ required\ deposit\ = initial\ margin\ requirement\ per\ contract\ \times \#\ of\ contracts$$

$$Total\ required\ deposit\ = \$6{,}220\ \times 6\ = \$37{,}320$$

38. A: An investor is awaiting significant news regarding the gold supply. Given the significance of the expected news, the result could be either an extreme price move up or down. The investor will want to profit from any extreme move in the price of gold that may result from this announcement. With this, the investor's best investment move would be to purchase a straddle. This strategy will allow him or her to best capitalize on the potential volatility that may result from the upcoming news on gold. Ultimately, when determining whether to purchase a straddle, this investor must not only consider their potential maximum loss but also the potential maximum gain and breakeven.

39. B: A customer who has received a call for additional margin to be deposited into his or her account can obtain the required equity to restore the account by transferring funds from an additional account, liquidating futures contracts, or depositing additional funds obtained from the bank. They cannot obtain the required equity through a loan from the futures commission merchant. There are no loans made for customers who are purchasing commodities.

40. C: If this investor had only purchased the 1 December silver 1500 call at 5, the maximum loss would have been 5.

$$5 - 2\ = 3$$

By also selling the 1 December silver 1700 call at 2, he or she has reduced the maximum loss from 5 to 3.

41. D: A maintenance margin is the minimum equity a customer is required to maintain to hold a futures position open. Falling below this margin requires a deposit by the customer to restore the account to the initial margin requirement. Negative price changes will cause the margin balance to fall.

42. A: "Marking to the market" is the process by which a futures commission merchant will monitor the equity of a margin account for changes that may occur due to changes in a futures contract price. "Corner" involves the accumulation or control by some parties of such a large portion of a commodity supply that they are capable of dictating or even manipulating the price. "Limit up" is the maximum amount, within a single trading day, a contract can go up or down. "Offset" is when an open futures position is closed out.

43. D: An option's premium is a measure of its value. Factors in determining the amount of that premium would include the supply and demand for the contract in the market, the volatility of the underlying futures contract within the market, and interest rates as they may dictate overall price movements within the market.

44. A: A bull call spread involves an investor purchasing a call with a lower strike price and simultaneously selling a call with the higher strike price. The investor believes that futures contract prices will increase, NOT decrease, and utilizes this strategy to offset the possible loss of the premium paid for the long call. A bull call spread is considered a debit spread also.

45. D: The bakery is concerned that prices on wheat may increase dramatically over the next several months due to a shortage in supply. If the bakery waits to purchase the wheat it needs, the company risks significant price increases. The bakery could purchase wheat in the spot market, take delivery of it, and then store it for the next few months. Doing so could lock in the current spot price for wheat and stave off risk of a price increase, though this will need to be weighed against the costs of storing and insuring such wheat. The company could also purchase wheat futures for September delivery. Here, the bakery is locking in the price paid for wheat in advance without paying any storage costs. So ultimately, the choice depends on comparing the storage costs of wheat to the premium the bakery would pay in purchasing wheat futures rather than the current spot price. Since the question does not provide this information, the best answer is that the bakery should either do B or C.

46. B: A diagonal spread is one long option and one short option of the same class and with different expiration months and strike prices. A calendar spread is one long option and one short option of the same class and with different expiration months. A price or vertical spread is one long option and one short option of the same class and with different strike prices.

47. D: A speculator can be a large fund as well as an individual investor. The goal is to profit from "speculations" regarding future commodity price movements, and the strategy involves injecting risk capital into the futures market. They do NOT seek to minimize or eliminate risk. That in fact is the objective of a hedger.

48. B:

$$\mathbf{78.0 - 75.5 = 2.5}\ \boldsymbol{loss\ per\ barrel}$$

Given that each crude oil contract represents 1,000 barrels of oil:

$$Loss\ per\ contract = loss\ per\ barrel \times 1{,}000\ barrels$$

$$Loss\ per\ contract = \$2.50 \times 1{,}000 = \$2{,}500$$

$$Loss\ of\ all\ contracts = loss\ per\ contract \times \#\ of\ contracts$$

$$Loss\ of\ all\ contracts = \$2{,}500 \times 2 = \$5{,}000$$

49. C: Long hedgers purchase futures to protect against the risk associated with a commodity price increase, NOT decrease. They could be users of the commodity or someone who does not own the commodity but who is contractually obligated to deliver it. They are considered "short the basis" if they are in a position to be obligated to deliver the physical commodity.

50. A: To be purchased and sold, all futures contracts require a margin account. The amount required will vary from contract to contract in that it's based on a percentage of the total contract value. A customer having purchased a futures contract will observe the margin balance increase as the contract price increases. To ensure that a customer's margin balance remains above its minimum maintenance level, the futures commission merchant will be observing the futures contract's price movement.

51. B: Hedgers do NOT seek to specifically profit from futures contract positions. They are users or producers of a commodity seeking to reduce business risk. They utilize futures to take the position that is opposite whatever their position in the underlying commodity is and utilize profits made from futures contracts to offset the effects of adverse commodity price changes.

52. C:

$$Loss\ per\ contract\ = per\ contract\ loss + commission\ charge$$

$$Loss\ per\ contract\ = \$2{,}500 + \$40\ = \$2{,}540$$

$$Total\ net\ loss\ = loss\ per\ contract\ \times \#\ of\ contracts$$

$$Total\ net\ loss\ = \$2{,}540\ \times 2\ = \$5{,}080$$

53. A: Treasury bill futures options are based on $1 million, NOT $100,000, par value of a 13-week Treasury bill. The premium is quoted as annualized percentage of that $1 million par value, and because of the four 13-week quarters in a year, it must be divided by four to determine the final amount owed by the investor.

54. C: An "in the money" call would involve the futures contract price being greater than the strike price. An "out of the money" put would involve the futures contract price being greater than the strike price. An "at the money" put would involve a futures contract price equaling the strike price. An "in the money" put would involve a strike price that is greater than, NOT less than, the futures contract price.

55. B: A short hedger may be someone who actually owns the commodity or the producer of the commodity. A commodity producer would be considered being "long the basis." A short hedger will sell futures to protect against the risk of a decrease, NOT increase, in the commodity price.

56. D: The maximum loss on a long straddle is limited to the total premium paid. The total premium equals the call premium plus the put premium. The maximum loss occurs only when the futures contract price at expiration equals the strike price of both the call and put options, and both options expire without being exercised.

57. C: The breakeven on both a short straddle and a long straddle equals the strike price plus or minus the total premium. A short straddle's maximum loss is unlimited, and a long straddle's maximum gain is NOT the total premium. It's actually unlimited.

58. D:

Price Spread:

Long 1 September corn 350 put

Short 1 September corn 250 put

Diagonal Spread:

Short 1 March wheat 75 call

Long 1 April wheat 60 call

Diagonal Spread:

Short 1 June gold 700 put

Long 1 August gold 850 put

Calendar Spread:

Short 1 May silver 1100 call

Long 1 October silver 1100 call

59. C:

$$Profit\ per\ ounce\ = 1{,}785 - 1{,}779\ = 6\ = \$6\ per\ troy\ ounce$$

Each gold contract represents 100 troy ounces.

$$Profit\ per\ contract\ = profit\ per\ ounce\ \times 100\ ounces$$

$$Profit\ per\ contract\ = \$6\ \times 100\ = \$600$$

$$Total\ profit\ of\ all\ contracts\ = profit\ per\ contract\ \times \#\ of\ contracts$$

$$Total\ profit\ of\ all\ contracts\ = \$600\ \times 5\ = \$3{,}000$$

60. B: The relationship between an option's strike price and the price of the underlying futures contract does NOT contribute to the overall profitability of the option position. The profitability of a position is impacted by the amount of the premium paid or received. An "in the money" call option has a futures contract price that is greater than the option strike price. An "at the money" put option has a futures contract price that is equal to the option strike price. An "out of the money" call option has a futures contract price that is lower than the option strike price.

61. A:

$$Total\ premium\ = call\ premium + put\ premium$$

$$Total\ premium\ = (.45\ \times 100) + (.41\ \times 100)$$

$$= 45 + 41\ = 86$$

$$Breakeven\ for\ call\ side\ = call\ strike\ price + total\ premium$$

$$Breakeven\ for\ call\ side\ = 200 + 86\ = 286$$

$$Breakeven\ for\ put\ side\ = put\ strike\ price - total\ premium$$

$$Breakeven\ for\ put\ side\ = 200 - 86\ = 114$$

62. D: An investor, by purchasing a long straddle, is not bullish or bearish when taking this position. They are anticipating extreme volatility in the futures contract price with moves toward either direction. Accordingly, they will simultaneously purchase a call and put on the same futures contract. This position will involve the purchase of two options with both the same expiration months and same strike price.

63. B:

$$Maximum\ gain\ on\ bull\ call\ spread\ = difference\ in\ strike\ prices - net\ premium\ paid$$

$$Maximum\ gain\ on\ bull\ call\ spread\ =\ (50 - 35) -\ (6 - 2)$$

$$= 15 - 4\ = 11$$

The maximum gain will be realized by this investor if both options are exercised.

64. C: An investor who sells a put will always receive the contract premium as payment for providing the buyer of the put with the option contract. The investor's maximum loss will be limited in that the price of the underlying contract's fall is limited to zero. The worst-case scenario for this investor is in fact the contract price falling to zero. The buyer would then exercise the option to sell at the higher contracted price, and the seller would be forced to pay that price for a contract that basically has no value for resale.

65. B: When determining the profit or loss on a speculative futures position, an investor must consider the number of contracts, the number of units per contract, the price at which contract was opened, and the price per unit per contract.

66. A: Time spread is another name for a calendar spread. It is one long option and one short option of the same class with different expiration months.

67. B: A September 45 call, trading at $41, and with a premium of $3 is "out of the money." Given an option's intrinsic value is the amount the option is "in the money," this option would have no intrinsic value. The time value of this option equals its premium value above its intrinsic value and is the price that is paid for the "option" or opportunity to buy or sell at the contracted price. With that, its time value would be the option's entire premium value of $3 because the option has no intrinsic value.

68. D:

$$Breakeven\ on\ bull\ call\ spread\ = lower\ strike\ price + net\ premium$$

$$Breakeven\ on\ bull\ call\ spread\ = 40 +\ (10 - 7)$$

$$= 40 + 3\ = 43$$

69. C: A report regarding wheat production is due out in the next few days. March wheat is trading at \$3. There's an investor with no knowledge of whether the report will be positive or negative for wheat production. This investor should take the following position: Long 1 March wheat 300 Call at .25 and Long 1 March wheat 300 Put at .22. This straddle would provide the opportunity to profit from an extreme price move either up or down for wheat. An extreme move up in price would allow this investor to buy wheat at the lower contracted price and then sell at the current higher market price. An extreme move down in price would allow the investor to buy at the current lower price and sell at the higher contracted price. The Long 1 March wheat 300 Put at .25 would be profitable only if wheat prices took an extreme move down. The Long 1 March wheat 300 Call at .75 and Long 1 May wheat 300 Put at .70 position involves two options with different expiration months.

70. D: Price spreads are utilized in determining whether the investor will want to exercise the option or let it expire and whether the position has resulted in a net credit or debit. Price spread analysis will also provide the position's breakeven point and its maximum loss.

71. C:

Purchased 1 March corn contract at 45

Sold 1 March corn contract at 53

$$Profit\ = 53 - 45\ = 8$$

72. B: The put buyer's maximum loss is the premium he or she paid to the seller, and the put seller's maximum gain is the premium received from the buyer. Additionally, the put buyer's breakeven is the contract's strike price minus the premium. The intent and hope in selling the put is to have it expire and NOT be exercised. With that, the seller would receive the maximum gain, the premium paid by the buyer, and no loss.

73. C:

$$\mathbf{1.16\ = 1\frac{16}{64\%} \times \$100,00}$$

$$\mathbf{1.25\% \times \$100,000\ = \$1,250}$$

74. B: An investor who sells a short straddle position believes the price of the futures contract will trade with minimal volatility and without any significant moves up or down. Ultimately this investor is NOT concerned with whether the price of the contract will increase or decrease, but instead, the focus is on the level of volatility and the significance of the movement as it may go up or down. The investor's investment outlook is neither bearish nor bullish in that he or she has no firm belief in what direction the market will be going. This sort of investment position is usually sold after a period of high volatility. The belief is that price volatility will be leveling out in the near term from there.

75. A: An "in the money" call option has a futures contract price that is greater than the option strike price. Here the January gold 97 call (when January gold is trading at 109) is the "in the money" option. The owner of this call option could exercise the option to buy the underlying futures contract at 97 and then potentially sell it at its current price of 109 for a profit. The February wheat 70 call is "out of the money" (when February wheat is trading at 57) because the call option has a futures contract price that is lower than the option strike price. The October corn 45 call is "at the money" (when October corn is trading at 45) because the call option has a futures contract price that is equal to the option strike price. It is unknown whether the July silver 155 call is "in the money" due to the July silver trading price not being provided.

76. B:

$$\mathbf{2.5\% \times \$1,000,000 = \$25,000}$$

$$\frac{\$25,000}{4} = \$6,250$$

77. D: The basis is the difference between the cash commodity price and the near-term futures contract and is quoted as the relationship between the commodity price and the price of the futures contract. As the basis strengthens, it becomes more positive, NOT less positive, and the direction of spread change will either strengthen or weaken the basis.

78. B: S&P 500 futures contracts are the most efficient hedge against systematic, NOT nonsystematic, risk. They are appropriate for hedging a large, diverse portfolio and could be utilized by portfolio and pension plan managers. Profits from a short S&P position can help to offset loss due to a decline in portfolio value.

79. A: A commodity's crop year is the center point of its agricultural contracts. A commodity's crop year starts at harvest time and ends with the commodity's harvest period of the next year. A commodity's harvest period involves the time when the crop is mature enough to then be prepped for delivery. All producers of a given commodity are subject to the same commodity growing season. There are no regulations put in place to spread out the release of the supply of a given commodity to the market over a long range of time rather than all at once.

80. A: The appropriate pricing unit for live cattle is 40,000 pounds. Sugar is 112,000 pounds, and feeder cattle are 50,000 pounds.

81. B: Changes in open interest will confirm or contradict whatever trend is being observed in the market. Monitoring open interest is merely an additional tool used to forecast pricing and determine what move to make next. Higher open interest means higher liquidity in that contract, and higher liquidity means smaller spreads for the contract. A decreased open interest indicates that market participants are exiting.

82. C: In the event of a commodity supply shortage, the market for the commodity may become inverted. Backwardation occurs as demand for the commodity and for the near-term contracts increases. When this sort of pricing structure occurs, it is NOT a good time for selling distant futures contracts. The price of the commodity is already higher than the price of the more distant futures contract, and there is no opportunity for profit.

83. A: Commodity and futures contracts (near-term and distant) pricing usually all move in the same direction. There is an upward sloping relationship between the physical commodity and futures markets, with pricing for futures trading above the commodity price. As delivery dates extend further into the future, pricing for futures contracts increases.

84. C:

$$\$75,000,000 \times 1.7 = \$127,500,000$$

85. C: The exchange sets the maximum amount by which the futures contract value can change within a session of trading. This is the limit up-limit down rule, which is also known as the daily price limit. The exchange sets minimum price variation for a contract, which is the contract "tick" and is NOT based solely on the contract's pricing but also on the number of units covered by the contract.

86. B: US Treasury futures are traded on the Chicago Board of Trade (CBOT). The contracts are NOT backed by the US government and therefore are NOT obligations of the US government. The contracts cover $100,000 par value of US Treasury bonds with maturities of at least 15, NOT 20, years from the delivery date.

87. A: Systematic risk is NOT diversifiable given that it is inherent to the entire market and would not be affected by focusing investment on a specific company or industry. It is also viewed as market volatility. An example of systematic risk would be rising inflation in that the effects of inflation are widespread and not industry or company specific.

88. B: Sugar is the commodity that is NOT priced in units representing 5,000 bushels. Instead it is priced in units representing 112,000 pounds. Wheat, soybeans, and corn are all priced in units representing 5,000 bushels.

89. C: Commodity prices are usually at their lowest during the harvest period due to the increased supply that is released for sale at that time. During a normal market, the commodity contract price for the harvest month will be lower, NOT higher, than the month before it. Forecasted production for the next year relative to the current year impacts contract pricing. If the current crop is still abundant and forecasts for next year are lower, the current harvest month's contract may be priced higher than the month before it. In this case the forecasted future supply will be seen as lower, thus demanding a premium price for the later month's contract.

90. D: An exporter will experience risk when selling product overseas. The exporter would be concerned with the dollar rising relative to the foreign currency to be received as payment. If the currency value falls, it will be worth fewer US dollars, and the impact will be a reduction in the effective sale price of the good sold. The hedge he or she could utilize involves the exporter selling foreign currency futures. The exporter would be considered a short hedger if selling currency futures.

91. C: Cocoa is not priced in cents per pound, but instead is priced in "dollars per pound." All four of the answer choices are "soft commodities," but only cocoa is valuable enough to be priced in dollars per pound.

92. A: In a normal market, futures contracts pricing increases the further out delivery months go. Pricing for delivery months are considered to be trading at a "premium" to the commodity. Delivery months that are further out have higher pricing due to a carrying charge. As the delivery month draws closer, the commodity price and spot futures contract price will move closer together, NOT further apart. During the actual delivery period, the contract price will be the same as the commodity price.

93. A: S&P 500 stock index futures provide investors with broad exposure to the bigger market by placing one order. The market is highly liquid. Contracts trade in minimum increments of $0.10, but the contract value is $250 times the contract price, NOT $150 times the contract price.

94. B: A support pattern occurs when a commodity price is falling and new buyers, attracted by the lower pricing, provide the needed demand to prevent the price from declining further. A resistance pattern occurs when a commodity price is rising and new sellers, attracted by the higher pricing, provide the commodity supply into the market that will prevent the price from increasing further. A reversal pattern involves the commodity price making an extreme or significant change.

95. D: The Commodity Futures Trading Commission (CFTC) and the Chicago Board of Trade (CBOT) provide reports of the grain supply. They're published weekly to help forecast futures prices. Grain is accounted for as visible supply once it is moving off of the farm. Any change to the visible supply report is an indication of a potential surplus or shortage. If the supply is seen increasing, it could be indication of an impending price decline.

96. B: The visible supply grain report includes grains that are in transit, in storage elevators, and on loading docks. It does NOT include grain that stays on the farm.

97. D: The contract pricing characteristics that are specifically chosen with the production of that particular commodity in mind are the pricing increments, the amount of underlying commodity to be covered, and the expiration months that will be traded.

98. D: An investor should sell foreign currency futures if a political event occurs that results in an increase in political instability in that foreign country. He or she should buy foreign currency futures if a large quantity of a valuable commodity is discovered within that foreign country, there is a dramatic rise in that foreign country's stock market, or unemployment in that foreign country goes down.

99. C: Corn does NOT have delivery months that are structured as consecutive months for some varying extended length of time. The delivery months for corn contracts are March, May, July, September, and December. Natural gas, copper, and crude all have delivery months that are structured as consecutive months for some varying extended length of time.

100. C: Commodity users are long hedgers, NOT short. They need to acquire the commodity and, accordingly, would like the commodity price to go down. They would also like the basis to widen and the futures price to go up.

101. D: Technical analysis involves the usage of charts as a significant tool. Analysts will utilize patterns seen in past commodity price performance to forecast pricing direction going forward but will NOT examine the fundamentals of the commodity's market. Commodity usage will also not be considered.

102. B: A commodity's carrying charge is made up of interest expenses on borrowed funds, insurance, and storage fees.

103. C:

$$\frac{126{,}000}{8{,}000} = 15.75$$

It's not possible for this farmer to sell 15.75 contracts. The question then becomes what the appropriate amount to sell is to best hedge the entire crop. He or she should sell 16 contracts.

104. D: When managing portfolios with holdings included in a variety of indexes, futures in those indexes can be utilized to hedge risk. The indexes here that could be utilized to hedge such a portfolio are NASDAQ 100, Russell 2,000, and Nikkei 225.

105. C: In a market where open interest is going up and the price of the commodity is also increasing, a strong, NOT weak, market would be indicated. If the commodity price is falling, new market participants are dominated by sellers, which would drive prices lower. If the price of commodity is increasing, new market participants are dominated by buyers driving prices higher.

106. B: A hedge's profit or loss has an effect on a commodity's selling price. The profit from a commodity producer's hedge will increase the commodity's effective selling price, and any gains from a commodity user's hedge will reduce the commodity's effective cost. Timing for when to establish a hedge is critical to its effectiveness, as is knowing when to remove a hedge. The time and price at which the hedge is removed is critical to its effectiveness.

107. A: Currency hedges are utilized by those who do business internationally. Currency value changes can impact profits and costs. A strong dollar is good for buying goods from overseas. A company purchasing products overseas might purchase foreign currency futures as a long hedge. Businesses needing to make payment in foreign currency will fear the value of the dollar going down, NOT up.

108. C: A reversal pattern indicates a significant commodity price change in trend. A bearish reversal shows the end of an upward trend and start of a new downward trend. A head and shoulders top is bearish in that it describes the reversal of an uptrend. A head and shoulders bottom reverses a downtrend, and is bullish.

109. D: The chart pattern that indicates buyers and sellers looking to trade a commodity at virtually the same price is called a consolidation. A support pattern occurs when a commodity price is falling and new buyers, attracted by the lower pricing, provide the needed demand to prevent the price from declining further. A resistance pattern occurs when a commodity price is rising and new sellers, attracted by the higher pricing, provide the commodity supply into the market that will prevent the price from increasing further. A reversal pattern involves the commodity price making an extreme or significant change.

110. B: A hedger would be seeking to protect against an interest rate drop and what that might mean to the investment he or she is intending to make at a future time. If interest rates drop, the price of outstanding bonds rises. If the price of the bonds goes up, the investor would have to pay more for the bond and then have a lower current yield and lower yield to maturity. A hedger could buy Treasury bond futures and establish a long hedge.

111. D: Open interest is the total of outstanding contracts that have yet to be closed or offset. It acts as an indicator of a market's strength and aids in signaling future market direction.

112. C: Nonysystemtic risk is what you assume in any particular security or position. Systematic risk is inherent in the market as a whole. Nonysytematic risk can be diversified away by purchasing different securities or buying from different issuers.

113. D: None of the above is actually true. When a commodity's price is less than price of futures contract, commodity has negative, NOT positive, basis. When a commodity's price is greater than the price of a futures contract, commodity has positive, NOT negative, basis. As the spread moves more negative, the weaker, NOT stronger, the basis actually becomes.

114. B: "Front month" would be described as the futures contract with the earliest delivery date, the one that is the most quoted, and the one with the highest amount of trading volume.

115. A: A commodity producer is a short hedger, NOT a long hedger. He or she sells futures to protect against the risk of prices going down. He or she is long the commodity and, with that, would like the commodity price to increase. He or she would also like the basis to become less negative.

116. B: Portfolio managers may hedge based on their portfolio's beta. A portfolio's beta-adjusted value is found by taking the value of the portfolio and multiplying it by the portfolio's beta. A portfolio's beta is its projected rate of change as it is relative to the market as a whole, NOT a specific segment of the market. A beta greater than one has volatility level that is higher than market, and a beta less than one is considered to be less risky.

117. C: Interest rate hedgers may be motivated by a need to borrow money at a future date through bond issuance. They would be hedging against the risk of interest rates going up. Short hedging here could involve selling Treasury bond futures.

118. D: Futures contracts can hedge a variety of financial risks. Corporations may use futures contracts to hedge interest rate risk. An import/export business could use futures contracts to hedge currency risk. Portfolio managers might utilize them to hedge the risk associated with a stock market price decline.

119. B: "Basis grade" is the minimum or standard level of quality that constitutes proper delivery in settling a futures contract.

120. A: In a market where open interest is going down, if the price of the commodity is also decreasing, a strong, NOT weak, market will be the result. If the price of the commodity is also increasing, short positions are being covered faster than the start of new positions. If the commodity price is falling, the result would be a liquidating market.

Share Your Story!

It's Your Moment, Let's Celebrate It!

Share your story @mometrixtestpreparation